Spiritual Mechanics

The Nuts and Bolts of Reality

Spiritual Mechanics
The Nuts and Bolts of Reality

Copyright © 2025 by Vishrant. All rights reserved.

No part of this book may be reproduced, stored in a retrieval system, or transmitted in any form or by any means, including electronic, mechanical, photocopying, recording, or otherwise, or translated into any language, without prior written permission from the author and publisher, except for brief quotations used in reviews or articles.

ISBN:
978-1-7638511-0-8 - ebook
978-1-7638511-1-5 - paperback
The Vishrant Buddhist Society

Disclaimer

This book is intended for educational and informational purposes only. The insights and teachings shared within this book reflect the personal experiences and understandings of Vishrant and are not intended as professional advice. The content of this book should not be used as a substitute for medical, psychological, legal, or financial advice. Readers are encouraged to use their discernment and seek professional guidance where necessary.

The author and publisher make no representations or warranties regarding the completeness, accuracy, or applicability of the teachings presented. The journey of self-inquiry and spiritual awakening is deeply personal, and each individual is responsible for their own path and experiences.

Contents

Introduction 5

From Suffering to Enlightenment 7
It's Just a Dream 13
True Maturity 31
The Spiritual Ego 51
Unconditional Surrender 59
Conscious Business 71
What is Surrender? 87
Relationships 93
Sangha – Jewel of Consciousness 113
Restful Yoga 125
Self-Acceptance 129
How to Deal with Shame 151
What Happens in Enlightenment? 171
We are One 183

About Vishrant 201

Introduction

The sky turns from baby blue to amber and gold as the sun slowly drops over the Indian Ocean off Perth's coastline. Up in the hills to the east of the city's expansive suburbs, the time for Satsang draws nearer. Western Australia has been blessed, but most are not aware of it; an open secret to the end of suffering and a doorway to freedom and bliss has been opened.

Vishrant can initiate people into the reality that exists before the world of dream; Sat-Chit-Ananda – Truth-Consciousness-Bliss. Vishrant is living as Beingness, which is before the dream of who we think we are. Vishrant is the embodiment of enlightenment and he radiates a beautiful energy field because of it. He has, however, not left the world. His teachings are pragmatic, with a comprehensive understanding of what is needed to raise consciousness and end suffering. His teachings include the nuts and bolts for the removal of ignorance and suffering in our busy, day-to-day lives.

Vishrant teaches people how to end suffering, find true love, live beautifully in relationships with others and ultimately, when they are ready, how to awaken from the dream of 'me' to a blissful truth of eternal peace.

Seekers travelling from all over the world, on all stages of their journey, come to the rolling hills of Perth to sit in his divine presence and hear his crystal-clear teachings. They are brought together by a curiosity or thirst for seeking the essence of Buddhism, the ultimate truth, our own true nature, freedom itself.

People sit down and meditate. Vishrant walks into the room and lights it up with his presence. "Hello everybody," he says, as he walks to the front of the room. He takes his seat and a warm silence fills the room as his hands come together to Namaste.

Everyone returns the gesture and after a moment of silence, he welcomes everyone: "Welcome to Satsang."

This book is a transcript of a series of Satsangs (talks) with Vishrant. Satsang is a Sanskrit word meaning 'to be in association with truth' or 'meeting in truth' and is traditionally held by an awakened teacher in a question-and-answer format with students. May the discourses and dialogues in this book inspire you to investigate the nuts and bolts of your mind and to seek the truth of what you truly are.

From Suffering to Enlightenment

> Surrender will set you free,
> That's the only thing that will set you free.
> Nothing else will.
>
> VISHRANT

V: *dialog from Vishrant*
S: *dialog from student*
~ *separate dialogues from different speakers*

V: Welcome to Satsang.

Unless you wake up to your true nature, you're lost. You may not think you are but you are, because living as an ego is not living as reality. The saddest thing to happen to a human being is to live as an ego because the ego is not programmed for happiness; it is programmed for misery, hence the suffering on the planet. You don't see animals suffering like humans do. Humans are just suffering machines because they are constantly wanting what they haven't got or wanting to change what they do have and are constantly getting attached to what they have and fearful of losing it. The only way out of this is enlightenment, which is to know yourself as truth. My life is dedicated to helping people get out of unconsciousness so they can get free because if you look around at the world, everybody is suffering. A lot of people pretend to not be suffering but their energy fields show what's happening inside them.

Higher consciousness will set you free from a lot of suffering; super consciousness will completely set you free. There is nothing more important than this.

I was speaking about the intricacies of watching the mind last night; it is not about watching psychologically, it's not about being involved in psychology, and it's not about analysing. It is about having a separate witness of the mind so you can see what the process of the mind is, not the psychology of whatever story you are lost in – that's all rubbish.

A lot of people get stuck in the story, analysing it and, of course, their consciousness levels stay the same until they die. It's not about analysing the mind's story; that's psychology, that's not what watching the mind is about. As a matter of fact, that's the opposite of it. That's still indulging in dreaming, and that's for the lost, the unconscious. If you want to get free of the mind, you need a silent witness that sees everything that's happening. What are you avoiding? That's always a good place to start: instead of starting with what the content of the story is, it is starting out before the content. The story is usually generated to avoid something, and the story is not real – it's dream. There's nothing real about story, there's nothing real about emotionality and there's nothing real about logic for that matter. The rational mind is not the answer. Having a witness to the mind is the answer. Having that detachment to see everything underneath the story – that's the answer.

Everything that is done here is to help people get free; everything that's said is to help people get free. There's no other reason for me to be here. Watching so many people suffering now and for so many years, seeing them indulge in it, indulge in resistance to life, indulge in a ton of stories that hurt them and quite often hurt others, rather than just developing the silent witness that sees the activity of the mind.

Getting involved in the psychology, getting involved in the story, is just dreaming. It is still the place of the lost, not the place of the seeker. It is true I studied psychology but with a silent witness developed from meditation watching the mind. If you haven't developed that silent witness that sees what the mind is doing, you haven't started yet, and getting involved in psychology is a waste of time. It is just another story that you'll indulge in and hurt yourself in and it goes on and on and on and on.

When you develop a silent witness, it sees the problem and the answer to every problem is surrender, the answer to every problem is acceptance, and then it's over. It does not think about it, does not try to work it out. That is just you indulging in suffering. Unless you have this silent witness, you don't see what it is you actually have to do. You're lost in a dream and you think the dream is you being conscious when you are analysing psychology. That is not conscious; that is being lost in dream.

You have to be separate; you have to have that detached witness. There isn't a thing that happens in my mind that is not seen because there is a silent witness there all the time that was developed 30-odd years ago. I love reality, not dream because it's where people hurt themselves. People get ungrounded, do stupid things and make bad mistakes. Love reality; unfortunately, reality doesn't have soft edges. It's actually quite hard because it's real. Soft edges are created by the cloud of dream that you wrap around everything. That's not real. The truth has hard edges; it's not soft and fluffy. The dream you might wrap around truth has soft edges because it's cloudy but it's not real. Love reality; don't like the bulldust. The seeker has to love reality, rather than bulldust. If you don't have a silent witness, it's quite possible you don't see the difference.

Satsang happens 24 hours a day, seven days a week for those who are interested in getting free. That means there's a light for those who want to get free. The dream of a life was given up completely so this light could be here, the same as my teacher did. You look into my eyes and you won't see any haze, you won't see any uncertainty, you won't see any fear, because it's not there. It's gone, and you are welcome to come so you can be free. The mind is a prison, it's a place where people suffer, and it's up to you. The door can be opened for you and you can be shown the way through but only you can step through.

It's up to you; the door is always there to be opened for you but most people don't step through. Most people avoid it and go back into their heads trying to work it all out. There's nothing to work out: the answer is surrender, the answer is acceptance, that's it. There is no other answer. Meditation brings you to the understanding of this answer. You want to be happy? You've got to get out of your head; it's not where happiness dwells. It's actually a suffering machine. It's up to you.

~

S: The studying of psychology and counselling, is that just a matter of developing skilful means to apply what you can see?

V: No. Being able to see your mind and take it apart is important. If you haven't got a silent witness, the study of psychology isn't going to help you much. Having met so many psychiatrists, so many psychologists, so many counsellors who are just miserable, who've studied psychology to the nth degree, yet are still miserable, it's clear that psychology doesn't help; having a silent witness of your mind helps.

S: Did the study of psychology help you apply what you saw in meditation in terms of skilful means?

V: It helped me make millions of dollars. Millions of dollars do not make you happy.

S: So, to be happy, I just have to be able to get out of my head – that's it? But to do that I would need…

V: No, you need to wake up actually. Have a look at what the Buddhist definition of happiness is – Sat-Chit-Ananda. Happiness for no reason: Truth-Consciousness-Bliss and that's when awareness is on awareness. That's the experience for the mind, of enlightenment.

~

S: It feels like the unwillingness to feel (emotional pain) is one of the main reasons why I'm not happy.

V: Yes, then your mind just scrambles around looking for and trying ways to not feel. Quite often, by blaming situations or other people, which creates more wounding because victim- orientated thinking creates more wounding.

S: Yes, last night you detailed how almost always the story will be victim-orientated because it's a way of people not taking responsibility for their feelings.

V: Yes, that's right. People don't want to feel something, so they find something or someone to blame for it. They may blame themselves for it but it is still the blame game. Anything to avoid feeling what's underneath and, of course, they don't even realise there's something underneath because they're too unconscious. They don't have this detached witness.

~

S: I just really need to practise self-acceptance. I keep finding different ways of getting self- acceptance outside of me.

V: The best is to be okay with not being accepted. I've been okay with not being accepted my whole adult life. You know why? I'm unacceptable. [LAUGHTER]. If you need acceptance from others, you're likely to twist yourself into some sort of knot; that's not you.

~

S: I just feel everyone's pain this morning; I don't really have any stories running.

V: It's felt here every morning because everyone's putting out pain around me; energy flows from full to empty always. An empath is someone who can feel you. A true empath can feel everybody because there are no defence systems in the way or filters to stop that from occurring. As you open up more and more and more, the chance of this happening to you is there and you've got to make it okay to feel pain because being around human beings is actually painful for someone who's wide open. Human beings, particularly westerners, are full of pain. It's why Osho Rajneesh designed Kundalini and Dynamic meditations because he recognised that all the westerners that were coming to him were full of pain. They needed a form of meditation to help release it and both Dynamic and Kundalini were designed to release pain from the body before sitting.

~

V: When you're a student of an enlightened teacher, you're in service to the teacher and the teacher is in service to you. It's a two-way service deal: the teacher is serving you by helping you raise your consciousness levels and you service the teacher in any way you can. This is traditionally how the masters and disciples have always operated. The students basically come with nothing except their pain. The teacher slowly takes their pain off them, opens them up and starts to show them the truth of their true nature.

Usually, the disciple finds a way to feed the teacher, and this is how it's happened for thousands of years. Both are in service: one is the master, the other is an apprentice but both are in service to each other and this relationship becomes a love relationship. Not a physical love relationship, but a love affair; the same love affair the teacher is already in and in that love affair, the student learns to surrender.

It's Just a Dream

V: The sight of creating an environment in which people can raise their consciousness, and as a result, end their suffering and find freedom from their minds is never lost.

That's been the goal now for over 20 years and it's a difficult task because people forget why we're here; people forget they're into higher consciousness. Never forget, not even for a moment. It's really clear that the only thing here that will help anybody is higher consciousness. Remaining in lower consciousness is suffering, and helping people remain in lower consciousness keeps them in suffering.

The endeavour to build a society is really building a vehicle, like a car or a bus, to take people into higher consciousness. This Buddhist society is a vehicle, and the society's activities are about building a very strong vehicle that can take people into higher consciousness, devoid of belief systems, ideologies; just a way of life with practices that will enable people to become free. For this, others are encouraged to help. It's a difficult task because people keep forgetting why they're doing it because they're too unconscious to realise what it's all about.

If you don't raise your consciousness levels, you're going to stay the same as you are until you die. That's how it is for all human beings. In raising your consciousness levels, you can see what's in the way and you can get free. Everything that is done here, is to enable that.

Some people over the years have been helpful; some people have actually worked in the opposite direction, usually to protect their own egos because they were too frightened to feel what was inside of them. All awakened teachers, all awakened people tend to be in the same game: Trying to help people get free. A lot of people who try fail, it's just how it is, the reason they fail is pretty simple. The willingness to be total is not there.

I used to see higher consciousness as being switched on; most human beings are actually switched off. They actually don't see what's happening around themselves very clearly at all because they're too interested in their own thoughts; they're too interested in their own mind, which is a closed-circuit television set, a dream in fact. As a result, the only way they can meet other people is through projections. In other words, what they think is happening rather than what is actually happening. This is lower consciousness; there is nothing conscious about projection. The way to get out of projection is to stop projecting and to start seeing what is actually happening.

It's difficult. Human beings dream. Present moment awareness to reality was developed to get free of the dream so others could be helped to find that too. The problem with being real, in other words living as reality, is that you are extremely dangerous to the dream. The dream likes to be soft and fluffy and safe. It also believes itself to be real but it's not; nothing you think is real. Nowhere you think you're going is real, nowhere you think you've been is real. This is all dream but it seems real to people. There's nothing real about it though. Once you hit reality and start living in the moment you see clearly, it's all rubbish, it's just dream and most people live in it. They don't like actually being around people who live in reality because reality takes the dream away. This is why, in a lot of ways, someone who's awake is a murderer: they murder the dream, they don't murder the human. They murder the dream because they take it away. As a result, quite often, they're attacked themselves… quite regularly. Gautama the Buddha himself had several assassination attempts upon him.

People who live as truth and who tell the truth, aren't popular to those who are dreaming; the dream has an investment in continuing to dream. The dream will sabotage the truth because it's uncomfortable or it will try to kill the truth because it's inconvenient. So, a lot of the big teachers don't really tell the truth, they water it down so those who are dreaming can handle it; they water it down so much that it's probably not even helpful.

Nothing that you think is real; nothing you think about yourself is real. Who you think you are is totally not real. See, that's a little bit hard for people who are dreaming to take, but take away your imagination and who are you? What are you? Imagination is not real, not at all; you have to imagine yourself to be somebody. Someone who is living as reality is encountering that imagination in others and challenging it constantly.

It's uncomfortable to be around someone who is living as reality, they're not going to support your dream, not really. Why would they want to keep you in suffering when that is where you suffer? They're going to undo it in every way they possibly can because they have a love affair with truth and they know that unless you get out of your dream, you're going to suffer until you die.

People in the past have been asked for their assistance to help set up this society and set up Satsangs, asked for help to help others get free. Sometimes those people who've been asked have been close to me or in my immediate sangha. Unfortunately, when their pain comes up, they turn themselves into the enemy because they don't want to feel what is coming up, and they don't take responsibility. You're responsible for the pain you have inside of you; that's your responsibility. When you come into the buddha field, it will probably start to come out because the coping mechanisms that hold it in place will be dissolved to some degree.

The pain that's inside of you is actually trying to get freedom; it's trying to get out. You're holding it prisoner so when it comes out and you don't want to feel it, you try to repress it. People have turned the process into their enemy because they don't want to feel what's coming out of them; the pain which was developed before they even came to Satsang. So maturity is taught because it is only really a mature mind that will take responsibility for pain. Immature minds blame everything and everyone else for it.

Freedom is the goal; to be a light is the goal so that you can light this planet a little more because it's a very dark place full of dream and quite often painful dream. People suffer a great deal because people resist life in their dreams. Not that there is anything happening; they just make it up. Without resistance there isn't any suffering. So while trying to take your dream off you and from time to time, you may see me as your enemy but I'm just doing what you ask me to do. Helping you get free from something that is not real. It is your willingness that makes a difference, your thirst for freedom; nothing else will make much difference. You're dreaming. Get no-mind through meditation and you'll see that you're dreaming and that nothing you think is real.

~

S: You started your discourse with talk of us forgetting why we're here.

V: Yes, you forget why you're here; you forget that you came here because you want to get free and you want to experience yourselves as heart, and love, and Beingness. You forget.

S: That has been my experience for the last couple of months. Where I felt like I was clear around why I came here, it's almost as if I've gotten bogged down in my analysis and the psychotherapy side of this and stopped having a clear picture of what I'm here to do and I don't know why that changes my view of things. Do you know why?

V: Well, as you started to peel back the layers, you started to find discomfort inside of yourself, so your mind scrambled to understand it through psychotherapy. Pain is just pain. It doesn't need to be understood; there is a need inside of you to control that pain, so it tries to understand it in a vain effort to stop it.

~

S: You run silent and dead still inside. You're able to speak sometimes to great complexity very quickly but you don't leave silence and stillness. So, I'm wondering how without an editor in your head, like a voice checking that everything that is coming out of your mouth is okay, how do you know what you're going to say will make sense or have anything to do with the conversation?

V: There's no idea. My mind lives in a state of trust. It trusts what's going to come out will be okay, or not okay; it doesn't matter. There's no trying to be seen in a good light, there's no trying to be accepted or to become acceptable. There is only delivering the truth, to the best of my ability.

~

V: There is nothing more important than to be free, there is nothing more important than raising your consciousness, there is nothing more important and if we're talking karma, the highest karma you can gain is by helping other people to raise their consciousness. Which of course works the opposite way as well, getting in the way of those raising their consciousness is detrimental to your karma. Gautama the Buddha stated that the highest karma that can be achieved is through teaching the dharma and I agree.

~

S: I see many of these immature, victim-orientated roles. How do I be more willing to face my pain instead of blaming others?

V: The question is answered by the question itself; you're too immature. You see immature people usually won't allow themselves to feel discomfort and quite often when discomfort comes up, they'll find a way to blame someone or something else. This is immaturity. A mature role takes full responsibility for what's happening inside. I make myself feel, so the teaching of maturity is quite important in higher consciousness because, without maturity, people can't actually gain higher consciousness.

~

S: When you spoke to me yesterday, you said to me that it was like dealing with a teenager, that I was behaving like a teenager and I feel like I'm stuck there.

V: No, no, you keep yourself there. Claiming you're stuck there is, once again, you not taking responsibility for yourself, which is actually a choice because you're an adult, not a child. If you were a child, you wouldn't have a choice but you're an adult: you have a choice; you're choosing not to be mature because you know the difference between a mature role and an immature role. It's a choice.

~

S: Today, I had the opportunity to work with people teaching dance and counselling, but I don't have the ability to take people into the space, so how can I serve higher consciousness apart from inviting them to Satsang?

V: As a seeker before awakening, the service was teaching acceptance and living as an example of being a man, that is, an example of maturity to young men and old men because of the understanding that maturity is a requirement. Also directing people to Osho, my teacher then, because sitting with an awakened teacher greatly benefits a seeker in their quest for awakening. As a psychotherapist, the service was teaching people how not to suffer by teaching them acceptance, maturity, and openness.

~

S: So, I don't deal with my pain very well and I will protect my right to be how I am. I get that I don't want to protect the immaturity, but I go unconscious and inherently protect the immaturity. I see you Vish, you're your own man and you say you do what you please, no one tells you what to say and how to be. I find I protect myself over the freedom to do that but it feels like a protection and it keeps me small. What is the impulse that drives me to keep wanting that?

V: Immaturity. In Paul Lowe's Mystery School, if you didn't comply with the rules, you were just asked to leave immediately, and all mystery schools have rules. This Mystery School has very lax rules compared to the mystery schools I've been involved in. It's not like you're giving up your individuality, but for a Mystery School to run successfully, there needs to be certain guidelines because people do come with their immaturity.

You don't tend to need guidelines with mature adults, but for immature adults, there has to be guidelines and there has to be consequences for when those guidelines aren't met. People can feel like they're being controlled, but they're not really being controlled, it's just that certain things have to be the way they are for it to work for everyone. An example is with Paul Lowe's groups in Italy in 1987. I was there for five months and if someone got angry, they were asked to leave, and they weren't welcome back. That guideline was pretty strict. There were a lot of other guidelines as well: we were in silence most of the time, and we were expected to do everything that was asked of us, and there was an agreement in that because we wanted to be in Mystery School. We were into higher consciousness and we had a teacher who was teaching higher consciousness, and higher consciousness was more important to us in the group than anything else. As a result of that group, consciousness grew, and grew, and grew. I was taught how to undo myself; how to meet pain in a way without escaping, to identify different methodologies that I used to avoid pain. Fortunately, as a mature man, it wasn't very hard. It was hard for some people. Maturity is just a requirement for higher consciousness.

In Osho's groups, wow, they were much stricter than here. All organisations need rules, need ways of being, and all organisations need leadership. If there isn't strong leadership, the organisation is doomed to fail. All leaders need to be able to stand alone, otherwise, they won't be able to lead, committees are rarely successful at leading, it's just the way it is.

How to be in the world, how to be in a society in a way that will bring success for that society which is a vehicle for higher consciousness: this is a very pragmatic way to operate; a way that will work. To be able to run any organisation, you have to be able to see the big picture the whole time. If you can't, you'll get lost in the small picture and the society will fail, as it will in business. In seeing the big picture, people can't see what you're doing because they're caught in the small picture and they think that is relevant, when it's only a very small part of a greater thing that is happening. As a result, leaders are often misunderstood, because they're seeing the big picture and operating from the big picture, and they can't explain to everybody every time they make a decision and quite often the people who are working with them can never see the big picture, because they're too caught in the story of the small picture.

In creating a vehicle for higher consciousness, there is going to be a great deal of opposition because the darkness is strong, and it has an investment in putting the light out. I don't know if I answered your question or not?
S: I'm gone...
V: Gone is my favourite.
~
S: I spoke to my brother today, and he's very crippled by fear and low self-worth, and it's like I'm the same as him, except I step through it because I'm here. I haven't healed my low self-worth, so I don't know how to help him, and I just left the conversation feeling very sad. If I don't love or accept myself how can I help somebody else?

V: It's very difficult because you don't know how to do it yourself. Someone who has healed their low self-worth, someone who has healed the wounds of their own heart, has a reasonably good chance of helping because they know how, but that healing really is reliant on your own willingness. So even after people are shown their wounding, and taught surrender and the way to heal, it quite often fails because they are not willing to feel what is there. They are not willing to face whatever is inside of them, and so it comes back to the person who has the wounding. It's their responsibility to become willing to feel whatever is inside of them. So even if you have the skill and you've healed your own wounding, it's probably unlikely you could heal your brother unless he was willing.
S: Yeah, he's not willing.
V: Then there isn't any chance. Only those who are willing can be helped; people who are not willing cannot be helped. In that way, we are responsible for our own consciousness, we are responsible for our own wounding, we are responsible for our own growth. It isn't in the hands of anyone else, it is us; we are responsible. Is there anything else?
S: Thank you.

~

V: As a psychotherapist, a lot of time was spent trying to get people to take responsibility for themselves.
S: Is that because without taking responsibility you can't…
V: Stop wounding yourself actually.
S: Ah, yeah.
S2: When people are in pain, and they go into a lot of victimness, they seem to create a lot of pain for themselves and it looks like there is no end to that suffering.
V: There is no such thing as an end, there is only now.
S2: When someone is being a victim, and consistently going into victimness, you know they're wounding themselves more. They're not healing themselves because they're wounding themselves more and so their pain comes up and they're hurting themselves more. It's worse than spinning their wheels.
V: Yep, victim-orientated people are full of pain.

S: When you're dealing with them, you just keep going? You just keep doing what you're doing?
V: Well, they may not be willing to feel their pain, but it's felt here for them, the pain comes into this me.
S: That sounds like your personal commitment that you follow and what they do is what they do and in that, it doesn't sound like there is much you can do. Aside from tell them and take their pain, someone's not going to change.
V: It is difficult, it's not easy. I can take quite a lot of people's pain out of them, mostly just with my students, but sometimes with people outside. If you sit with me, it's only a matter of moments before the pain starts coming in because pain is compressed energy and full always empties into empty. Over time, sitting with me cleans people quite nicely, but they may still start topping it up with victim-orientated thinking.
~
S: I felt really easily irritated today and I could acknowledge that I just felt hormonal or spikey because I think I started to get annoyed at things that don't normally irritate me.
V: Yeah, that's a good tell.
S: I felt like I just had to wait, like in a couple of days it will go away. Is that all I can do while I have PMS?
V: You have to be willing to feel your pain and then you won't be so reactive; a lot of the reactivity is an unwillingness to feel the discomfort. It's like you're flipping around like the worm on the hot tin roof trying to find something comfortable.
S: Yeah, the story and the pain could just possibly be irritation, or is it something…?
V: Well it could be, it's hard to say. You have to watch yourself and see. It's like operating as a masseuse: when you touch another human being, there is usually a massive transfer of energy. When we just stand close to them, quite often there's not that much unless they're really leaking out, but when we touch someone, we transfer all of our pain into them, or we take all of their pain off them, so it's relative to how full or how empty you are. In the Hindu religions, it's about becoming sattvic. If you are sattvic, you are empty and

then you can start to help people with their pain because you have the ability to take it out. Of course, as you start to take it out you feel it, so you feel their pain that they're unwilling to feel.

S: I did have another question; you spoke about leadership, something about standing alone to be a leader?

V: Yes, because people who can't see the forest and can only see the trees will quite often turn you into an enemy.

S: Yeah, so I just wondered, because I'm in a position of leadership, you were saying something about the people who are underneath you often can't see what the leader is meant to see or can see.

V: Yeah, it's like on a flybridge cruiser: the guy on the top deck steering the cruiser can see a lot more than the guy under the deck can see, you know? Who are you going to let drive the boat?

S: Sometimes I have to make decisions at work to make things work that inconvenience some of the staff. So then what do I do as a leader in that situation then? Do I try to explain?

V: Well, you can try to explain, but you do what you want because your job as leader is to take care of everything and everybody. You may actually get some non-acceptance from some people you cross, but that's part of the deal of being a leader, because you have to make decisions that don't make everybody happy, particularly with immature people who just want it their way. You've got to be okay with being not accepted, betrayed and lied about, often a fair bit.

S: So, did you just heal these one by one or did you...

V: Heal what?

S: Not heal sorry, but remove belief systems about not being betrayed, lied to...

V: Those beliefs systems were removed. I wasn't willing to spend that much time in resistance to life.

~

S: Earlier, you were talking to someone about personality or something like that, and I was wondering how do you distinguish between places where you're identified and defensive in order to maintain that identity and where it's just okay to have some differences in personality traits?

V: If you are with someone who's ahead of you, you can ask them because chances are you can't see. The other way of course is to develop a silent witness and have more clarity about your own mind.
S: I liked what you just mentioned about asking those ahead of you for what they can see inside yourself.
V: Well, if you can't see and you don't ask, that is arrogance, which is a form of stupidity. If you have the benefit of being with people who are further ahead of you, it's arrogant not to ask. What are you protecting by not asking?
S: I don't have an answer to that right now, but it's a good question.
V: It'll be low self-worth.

~

S: It feels like it's taken not having anyone around to blame for my pain, that I start to realise the pain was mine all along.
V: Yes, and you could have remained in blame when there weren't people around; people can stay in victim orientation whether there are people around or not, whether there's someone to blame or not because it's all imaginary. You can still hang on to bitterness and resentment, even though there are facts to the contrary. So many people do that. People who are very victim-orientated quite often don't like the truth very much.

~

S: I find that things like heart pain and obvious pain are more okay than this experience of pointlessness.
V: The pointlessness? That's just part of the pain. People think that pain is just pain, no. Emotional pain or pain body pain often have hopelessness or helplessness, and pointlessness is a part of that. Particularly in low self-worth, that's what makes it so icky. It's why most people try to avoid it. You have to be okay with being worthless to even really get in touch with it because, otherwise, you hold yourself away from it somehow.
S: Yeah, I try to fight it.
V: Yes, you try to fight it.
S: Okay, thank you.

~

S: You started your discourse talking about no-mind, and what I would like to be able to do is, amidst the drama or feeling lost and caught, just to be able to drop it.

V: Then you would need to become more conscious than you are because if you're conscious, it's all just story and you can drop it in a moment. That's the beauty of being conscious. The opposite occurs when you're unconscious; you can't drop it. You get caught in it, you suffer in it – that's unconsciousness. This is why higher consciousness is so beautiful; it affords you relief from that suffering. It's why higher consciousness is taught here. People are taught to become more conscious, so they don't have to suffer anymore. Anything else?

S: No, thank you.

~

S: I'm in a lot of pain.

V: So what? I'm in a lot of pain right now too. So what? It's not going to stop me from helping people. Not because of awakening, but because I am a man.

S: Last night, I was having an argument with my partner, and my partner said that the energy they were picking up from me was very irritated or agitated and they said it was probably something I picked up from work.

V: Was this after Satsang?

S: Yes, after Satsang.

V: You got that because of the conversation we had during Satsang.

S: Yes, and I guess where I go with that is, like… to me, it kind of discounts what I'm saying.

V: I understand that.

S: I feel like what I'm saying is logical or reasonable.

V: Yes.

S: And I feel like I'm having the point taken away.

V: Yeah, but you're not aware of what you're transmitting in your words. The Krishnas are very big on this; it's not just words, it's energy. As a matter of fact, the energy is more important than the words. In the Krishna religion, if you're in the kitchen and you're not experiencing love for people, you need to leave the kitchen because whatever energy you're carrying will be put into the food. This is

true, this is known to be a fact; whatever energy we carry, we put into food. Whatever energy we carry, we put into human beings, and so you may need to look at what you're transmitting besides logic.
S: Okay, so if I realise that I'm triggered and I'm transmitting irritated energy, do I just have to drop it in that moment?
V: It's not a bad idea. I would. Why would you want to fill someone you're trying to talk to with irritated energy – what kind of result do you think you're going to get with that? It's like when you're talking to someone and you're filling them up with anger energy, which is pain. What kind of reaction are you likely to get even if everything you say is logical?
S: Yeah.
V: It's not the words, it's not the story, it's the energy.
S: So, I can drop the energy and still address the point?
V: Well to drop the energy, you'd actually have to have the ability to drop whatever is going on inside of you to come back to zero. If you've actually wound yourself up to a state where you're aggravated or even angry, even if you go back to zero in your mind, you're still going to be carrying the energy for a while. Anger can hang around for hours after a person has dropped it. Anything else?
S: You were talking to me yesterday about my new job, and what's happening with the job, and you were pointing out that I was looking from a very small picture perspective and being selfish about the way I was approaching it. It wasn't until after you took me through the step-by-step process where I saw the bigger picture and was able, from that, to go, 'Oh, that makes sense.'
V: Why couldn't you see the bigger picture straightaway?
S: I was stuck in what I wanted.
V: You were stuck in selfishness, self-obsession. Selfishness in what you wanted, and people who are like that can't see the big picture. They miss it because they have too much of a filter on.
S: So, you have to be fairly conscious to be able to see that.
V: Or very mature. If you're mature, you don't get caught in victimness anyway. You're going to put others before yourself because that's a part of being mature. Only taking care of yourself is a giveaway of immaturity. That's what children do.

S: In a scenario like that, if you were to approach it from a bigger perspective, would that work?
V: No, you actually have to develop mature roles and operate in the world from mature roles and, carrying mature roles, you take care of everyone, not just yourself, and then you would have seen it. You were operating from an immature role, a self-obsessed role, so you couldn't see what was happening for them because it was all about you. Okay?

~

S: Yesterday and today on the phone when I was talking to you, you said I was purging.
V: Yeah, you are now actually.
S: Yeah, I thought about that the last two hours before Satsang, and as I was driving here, I was listening to you in the car.
V: Ah, that'll start it.
S: What is purging?
V: Purging is just where energy that has been repressed is leaving, that's all purging is. Does that make sense? Quite often, as it's leaving, it might affect how the mind thinks and feels.
S: I don't feel too different, like physically, I feel strange things in my head and chest.
V: Yes, you are purging, I can feel you. You actually have quite a strong mind and I think you can cut through things with your mind.
S: Yeah, I've just been remembering that thoughts are not real.
V: True, but I didn't mean that. I mean that you actually have a strong mind. You have quite a strong mind because you use your mind analytically regularly. It's quite strong and you can cut through energy with it. That's what I'm saying.
S: I still don't quite understand what you're getting at. I mean, is it good or bad?
V: It's neither good nor bad, it's just what is.
S: Um, does it hurt you when energy is coming out of me?
V: Yes, but my job is to help people get free, help humans get free and unfortunately, part of that job is actually feeling their pain.
S: Do I need to take more responsibility for what's happening?
V: No, you're doing okay. It's great that you're clearing; it's good news, not bad news. This stuff is better out than in. Anything else?

S: I feel like I start purging more after yoga?
V: Yes, you would, that's what the asanas are supposed to do; free everything up.
S: What should I be looking out for? You said that my mind, like my thinking, will be affected by the energy.
V: Yes, well it'll probably make you think negatively; quite often, people who have energy leaving them think negatively. It's like they have a filter over everything. Then again, maybe not, because you've got other things happening. Anything more?
S: I appreciate the topic of maturity tonight and also what you were saying about seeing the big picture. You were talking to someone about seeing the big picture versus being selfish and just seeing what you want.
V: It's the same in advertising, seeing the small picture and big picture.
S: So, the big picture is what are you selling? Is that what you mean?
V: The big picture is how it's going to affect everyone's mind, that sees every part of it, and how it'll affect them. That's the big picture.

~

S: You were saying last night that you can see the bigger picture because you are not interested in your own story.
V: Well, it's impossible not to see the big picture because I'm always in the big picture.
S: Yeah, sorry, I'm lost on that bit. When the story is gone, all that's left is to make everything work?
V: Well yes, that's right. The big picture is about making everything work, but that means you have to take everything into consideration, all the time.
S: All the time... I often go narrow-minded.
V: Small picture.
S: Yes, small picture, but my partner sees a bigger picture, and he helps me see the bigger picture.
V: That's good. Anything else?
S: No, thank you.

~

V: I'm constantly trying to get people to see the bigger picture, but because they can't get out of their own story, I can't show them the bigger picture.
S: It's been a pretty interesting Satsang.
V: Why?
S: Just the calls on maturity and how the reaction affects the community.
V: Yes, immature people, well the people who are assets to the community, are the mature people because they will make it work for everyone and people who are immature are liabilities; if there are too many of them in a group, they will destroy the group. A healthy group has quite a few mature people in it.
S: Yeah, because I haven't had any major roles for a while, I've just been doing my bits here and there.
V: Aha... Anything more?
S: Yeah, after work, just driving home, I just dropped back and could see the different dramas and points of happiness from throughout the day.
V: Oooh, nasty.
S: Yeah, it was quite easy just to let it go.
V: That's best.
S: Yeah, I could find a bit of distance.
V: Well that's good, having distance helps.
S: I just noticed being in a room of practising counsellors that most of them can't stay still.
V: Counsellors... yeah well, not many counsellors can stay still. You meet someone who can stay still, and you've met someone who has done the work on themselves. These guys haven't done work on themselves – they've just learnt something from courses and got a certificate. It doesn't mean anything; it's worthless as far as I am concerned. If you can't stay still because you're full of painful energy, well what do you think you'll be giving your clients? Maybe you can bring that up next time? Anything else?
S: You said to my partner that I can't confront?
V: Well it sounds like it.
S: What's in the way?

V: You're frightened of what's coming back because when you confront people, you can quite often get hostility and to avoid hostility, you don't confront.

~

V: We can make this society a great vehicle for higher consciousness. It will require your participation and your support: I'm putting my totality into it, I would like your support, it's up to you.

Thank you for Satsang, good to see you brave hearts here tonight.

True Maturity

V: One of the first things I studied in the way of higher consciousness was The Handbook to Higher Consciousness, a brilliant little book written by a guy called Ken Keyes, who was a paraplegic. His main message that was really, really essential for happiness and success in the material world was, "I make myself feel." In other words, no one else is responsible for how I feel, which means I can never be a victim, not really because I am aware that I make myself feel. Nobody can make me feel but me. Now that might sound really simple, but if you get it, it's just amazing. You can hear me, you can hear my words, but there isn't a person in this room who can actually hear me; I'm waiting still. You think that somehow the world affects you, that the world is responsible for your feelings, that other people affect you and are responsible for your feelings. As a 19 year old, I learnt this isn't true.

As long as you believe, and it is a belief – it's not a reality, that other people can make you feel then – you can be a victim and you will probably create stories when you get feelings about what they are doing, rather than realising that you're making yourself feel, that no one is making you feel. They are just doing what they do, saying what they say. Only you can make you feel. This is the ultimate in maturity. As a matter of fact, anything less than this is immaturity and it's the reason that most people don't wake up; they're not mature enough to support awakening. You make you feel, nobody else can make you feel. All your blame keeps you contracted in lower consciousness. You can't leave lower consciousness as long as you think the world and other people make you feel; not possible. You are 100 per cent responsible for how you feel.

I don't know why I got it, but I got it when I was 19, so I haven't really fallen into being a victim since, and as a result, rarely suffered. Victims suffer at their own hand because there is no such thing; you have to volunteer. Two people can have the same thing happen to them and one sees it just as it is, the other turns themselves into a victim of it. One suffers, one doesn't. It's a choice to volunteer to be a victim. Some people live their whole lives as victims, constantly blaming other people and situations for how they feel. These people are actually delusional because you have to volunteer to be a victim. Some of you might be scrambling right now thinking, "yeah I can hear him" but where is the proof? See, the proof is in your actions, in your behaviours, in how you live your life. That's the proof, not in what you think, in what you say. That's usually rubbish. If you know you make yourself feel, you don't get caught in the drama of blaming others for how you feel or creating stories about situations and others where somewhere inside it's not your fault.

It took me a long time to realise why people can't raise their consciousness levels above a certain point, and it's really bottom-line: maturity. Immature people don't take responsibility for themselves; they blame others and they stay in lower consciousness accordingly, and they suffer accordingly. "I make me feel"; you cannot make me feel. You can do outrageous things, but only I can make me feel. I am fully responsible for my feelings. The little talk I've just given is probably the most important talk you will hear in your life. It's where most people, 99.999 per cent, fail. I don't set the bar of maturity, I just happen to know where it is. How adult you are or how mature you are is up to you because you're the ones who are going to choose the roles you play. If you choose roles of being a victim, blaming others, blaming the situation, your maturity levels are low and you will suffer and you will probably try and include other people in your suffering because that's what immature people do; they actually try and hurt other people as well as themselves. Some of you are starting to doze off. The truth actually disturbs people so they go to sleep when they hear it. I don't think there is anything more important than the subject I am talking about tonight if you're interested in having a happy life, if you're interested in raising your consciousness levels. How mature are you? Or a better question yet, how immature are you?

~

S: You said that you didn't exactly know why you heard that so deeply when you were 19. Do you remember being a victim before then?
V: Oh, heck yeah.

S: Was it very dramatic for you when you found that piece of information?

V: I was so enthralled with that particular book, The Handbook to Higher Consciousness and the information in it that I read it about 21, 22 times in a row because every time I read it, it sunk in deeper and I got a little bit more out of it and I realised it was gold. The funny thing is the people who introduced the book to me had also read it, but they didn't think it was gold because they didn't operate it; they remained victims. They remained immature. Ken Keyes' insights would have come through satori; a deep, deep, deep understanding of how the mind works, and why.

~

S: You said you recognised the truth of it. What allowed it to permeate and change the way you saw things so deeply; why doesn't it have that effect on everybody?

V: I thought it did. I didn't realise that the other people weren't getting it.

S: What stops it? I feel like it makes sense, I feel like I can understand, it but it's not how I live.

V: That's true.

S: I see myself as a victim every day, and every now and then, I realise that's not possible, and then I'm still a victim.

V: All I can say is I was very conscious when I was 19.

S: So, it's just consciousness level, that's all?

V: Well, if your consciousness is high enough, you see things quite clearly. If your consciousness levels aren't high, you don't see much at all. People who live in drama don't see much at all. Their consciousness levels are so low, they have no clarity to see because they are constantly creating mess in their own minds with the drama that they run.

S2: After you realised this, did you have to practise removing victim-orientated thinking?

V: Well, I saw it, and then I removed it. Every time a victim-orientated thought arose, it was discounted as rubbish. At a later stage, all the belief systems that supported victim- orientated thinking were looked at and undone.

S2: When I feel bad, I tend to call that victim-orientated thinking.
V: Possibly… depends on what you're blaming for feeling bad. Some people feel bad and they create a story in their mind about something that is happening and turn themselves into a victim of that, not knowing that is just a feeling they are having. They create a story that they hopefully can solve because they are feeling something. Of course, solving that story isn't going to change that feeling because the feeling was there before the story.
S2: So where should I direct my awareness? Is it looking at the feeling itself?
V: No, you watch the mind and you don't support any form of victim-orientated feeling. We have a choice to support it or not, it's up to us.
S2: Does the mind create story to distract itself from feeling pain?
V: It usually creates a story in an unconscious effort to solve the uncomfortable feeling. The mind feels uncomfortable because something is arising or something has been touched so it creates a story that hopefully it can solve. It usually isn't true, but it involves other people, so other people get brought into the drama which isn't really happening, with all sorts of emotions that make it seem more real, but it's still not real. This is how they live. There is nothing happening, in fact, just a feeling; just some energy is arising, or someone's done something and it's triggered something, but even if something is triggered, it's your feelings. You're making yourself feel, not them.
S: If it is a trigger then that's a belief system?
V: Could be, could be a belief system in play. Ask the question from time to time, "How conscious do you want to be?" Because we're talking about consciousness levels here, if you can't see that you're being a victim, then you are unconscious.

~

S: This morning, I was a victim and my thinking was that I was expecting you somehow to take care of my needs and I need to be responsible for taking care of my needs so…
V: So, what was the feeling? I can help you if you want because I know the answer.
S: Discontentment.

V: Discontentment, that was the feeling...
S: And I wanted to make you responsible for my discontentment, so I was blaming you, but I just wasn't taking care of my own need.
V: Can I talk about that a bit? Okay, so there is a discontented feeling, and the discontented feeling was uncomfortable, so you created a story around it at an unconscious level to create a possible relief and you aren't quite conscious enough to see that.
S: I see that, but that's how it played out unconsciously and then what I recognize is I am trying to make Vishrant responsible for... whatever I said before [LAUGHTER] So I took responsibility. The damage was already done obviously, but the intention for taking responsibility, I had to carry that throughout the day, with every interaction with you to be mindful of not letting it rear up; making sure I'm taking responsibility. Is that just the continuation of the pain body or a feeling?
V: Usually, you justify your position, so you never see it.
S: But I haven't.
V: Not today, but you did first up, for a while, and then you saw it and you took responsibility for it, but that's actually why you haven't seen it clearly before, because you mitigate your responsibility, you have excuses for it.
S: Yeah and then I was absolutely direct with you around, this is what I've done: I've tried to blame you and make you responsible and taking care of something I've needed to take care of and it's almost like an expectation that you should know that this is what I need and it's not the case whatsoever.
V: No, it runs a little deeper than that though. There's more to it than that, it's not that simple.
S: Yes, but what I was trying to work on today was that point of trying to defer...
V: It's related to how you treat yourself inside of you. You have an internal bully and when you feel pain, you externalise that internal bully. If you didn't have that internal bully, you wouldn't be externalising it.
S: I have been reading about the bully in some literature over the last month, it's on my bedside table.

V: You have to be very conscious to see this stuff when it's happening, but that's the game we're playing; the game of consciousness.
S: Yes, sometimes I forget, and I just want to be in life.
V: This is life.
S: And around you, it's like conscious life.
V: This is life. Unconscious life is dream, it's not life, it's existing in dream. This is reality.

~

S: A tendency I have when I get caught or triggered on something is to lose consciousness and what I hear you saying is, you need to be really conscious.
V: Yes, that's right.
S: So how do you not…
V: Being conscious has to be more important than anything else, basically. It's a bit like when you get to higher levels of consciousness: you have to put truth first, every time, but at the lower levels of consciousness, you also have to put consciousness first and when you do that, then you put clarity first because without clarity there is no consciousness. People who don't have clarity for one reason or another can't see. They're in the dark.
S: Because you were particularly conscious as a young man, you didn't always get caught in lower consciousness when you got triggered. You could still see what was going on around you. How did you prioritise clarity and not keep getting caught? Why didn't you do what so many others do and just go down and down and downwards, more victimness, less clarity, more victimness, less clarity. How did you just stay clear, think, "Oh this sucks. I don't want to do this," and just stop it?
V: Because I was conscious enough not to go down. I had to pretend to others that I was at the same consciousness level that they were, and to me, I was running rings around everybody. That's why I had to leave Australia when I was 28 to find teachers because there was no one here that I couldn't run a ring around. The consciousness levels of the teachers here were too low. The game is consciousness, higher consciousness; this is the game that we are playing, this is what Buddhism is about, it's what Hinduism is about, it's what Tao-

ism is about, and it's what Sufism is about. In higher consciousness, no one can control you. While you're in lower consciousness, you can be led around by anybody, and you probably won't even know it.

~

S: I've been having a few encounters with my sister, not confrontational, just trying to take victimness off her after Satsang Friday night and then again today. Then she texted me, saying she stopped running thoughts today and I just felt gratitude for this. I can hear your teaching, even though I haven't changed it, well I've changed it a little bit, not to be a victim for the rest of my life.

V: What do you reckon that's worth? Look at all the suffering that's involved in being a victim. What's it worth to never be a victim again for the rest of your life?

S: It'd be worth living life without an arm or a leg or being in a wheelchair.

V: [LAUGHTER] you can't actually put a price on it, no? Victims' lives do not work; by definition, victims are helpless. Victims or people who see themselves as victims make themselves helpless; they turn themselves into victims.

~

S: I'm very grateful to have Satsang every day to pull me up whenever I'm running victimness and immaturity and also just the recognition of today when I got back after I went walking. You texted me when I was walking and I stopped immediately and took 100 per cent responsibility for my feelings and I noticed the shift; there was a distinct lack of crippledness or powerlessness. The experience was one of… I was mindful that there was a wariness and a nervousness around me, but I was like "hang on, I'm responsible for my own life and what's happening in it right now" and I feel like I didn't go down the chute and I maintained a buoyancy for the rest of the day. That's it.

V: To give you an idea of how hard it is to teach this, imagine trying to teach your brother this. Same programming.

S: I think it would be easier than my sister.

V: Yeah, the only way it's possible is with your willingness, nothing else.

~

S: When you said something like "what's it worth to not be a victim?"
V: Yeah, what's the value of that?
S: Yeah, it's priceless. Yesterday, I was talking to a client who I did a job for and she's having a hard time with the owner of her property, who's not happy with how an old part of the house is being maintained. I spoke to her yesterday and it was so painful, just on the phone talking to her because she was such a victim of what was happening with the owner. I was listening to her and I was thinking, "it's just what is" and yet, I do the same thing. I see it in her and I'm thinking "wow, that's painful", and then I go into resistance that someone didn't put enough paint on their roller or too much or someone looks at me funny. I still do it, so how do I hear so that I change me? How do I hear so I stop being a victim?
V: You actually don't want to.
S: Why?
V: Because you don't.
S: I want to be a victim?
V: Yes. People fight for their victimness, their right to be victims. Victims fight for their right to be victims; they insist that they are victims. Look and see. Take this woman that you're doing the cleaning for, try and take her victim orientation thinking off her and look at what happens to you. She would then try and hurt you. This is how unconscious the population actually is – people fight for their suffering.

~

S: Earlier today, I was doing a quote and sat down in the car to work something out and I had some sort of existential moment where I was like, why am I doing this?
V: Because standing in the car is uncomfortable [LAUGHTER]
S: I didn't have the clarity to see the answer like that. [LAUGHTER]
V: Because there isn't much headspace, your neck begins to bend, unless you've got a very tall car. I think Fred Flintstone could stand in his car, and Barney Rubble.
S: Yeah, they had very strong legs. [LAUGHTER] So I was sitting in the car and nothing profound happened for me, just this strange

question, but I did wonder: what motivated you to keep doing anything if there is no dissatisfaction driving you? Why bother?
V: I'm like a train that has been fired up with coal. Try stopping me.
S: What's the coal?
V: The love of truth.
S: Wow, that's quite different. I'm just driven by discomfort [LAUGHTER] That's good, thank you.
V: The operative word being love. Love is the most beautiful thing, it does not take prisoners, it is very sweet.
S2: I loved what you were just saying.
V: About standing up in the car?
S2: That's going to change my life. [LAUGHTER] know how much pleasure I get when I have the clarity to be able to explain something to someone, something I can see about higher consciousness and just realising when you were speaking...
V: ...Like that avocado up there is bigger. Higher consciousness. What sort of thing, you see? The thing about higher consciousness is that you can't explain it. Lower consciousness is living in knowledge, higher consciousness is not knowing. How do you explain that to those who value knowing?
S2: But there is still knowing how victimness is created, for example.
V: My mind is still right now, anything else?
S2: You say any negative thinking is victimness.
V: Not necessarily.
S2: With negative thoughts, you really need to look at the contrast between how things should be and how you want them to be or...
V: Victim orientation requires blame. Negative thoughts don't necessarily encompass blame.
S3: You posed the question earlier, "What would it be like to teach stopping victimness to your brother?" and it made me think instantly of my sister and how I have the exact same programming and the attachment to being an angry victim.
V: Ooh, that's awful.
S3: And I was trying to talk to her about victimness when she was in the state and she just couldn't fathom it at all.

V: No, not at all, most people can't.
S3: When I hear you talk like this, even though I make myself a victim, it's like I know that there's another way and I would have never known that if I didn't meet you.
V: That's true, well it's not necessarily true, someone else could have told you.
S3: Thank you.

~

S: I loved the talk. With self-blame, is it the same mechanism?
V: As being a victim of yourself? Yeah, the same. You can be a victim of three things, I've noticed: another person, the situation or yourself. All of it is rubbish, none of it is real. It is delusional thinking.
S: So, to stop self-blaming, is it to take responsibility?
V: Stop it. Is there anything else?
S: No, thank you.

~

S: I was talking to my brother tonight and he watched a movie called Limitless and he said he would love to have the clarity to be able to use all parts of his senses and brain to see things coming and going.
V: Well you can to some degree; not to the degree that they do in that movie, but you can get up there. You can read a whole room at once, you can feel what everyone is feeling at once.
S: Yeah, that's what came to mind, you, and what I was talking to you about recently. I want to be switched on like you, but there is so much story of me in the way.
V: Well closure keeps people very little and those people who are closed are very defended. Openness is the key to higher consciousness, but most people refuse to practise openness! They practise defensiveness and closure instead and then justify it. Anything else?
S: No, thank you.

~

S: I really liked the discourse because it's true what you said, I can't hear you and there will be moments of recognition, but it doesn't go very deep.

V: The karma to come into a Buddha's presence, but not the karma to be able to hear the Buddha. You don't have enough good karma to hear.
S: How do you accrue good karma?
V: You create good karma for yourself by becoming a giver instead of a taker. This is why most Buddhist teachers teach generosity. Selfish people create tremendous negative karma for themselves and suffer accordingly.
S: Yes, I can see that. I feel like I've done a lot for people.
V: You don't put yourself aside for your partner. Giving begins at home, not just with others.

~

S: I can't remember who you were talking to, but you said people fight for their victim- orientated thinking.
V: Yeah, you fight for your right to be a victim; you fight for your right to suffer. It's a bit silly, isn't it? But you watch, you watch people doing it.
S: Yeah, I can see how I do it. Why would I do that?
V: Because you're unconscious, otherwise, you wouldn't do it.
S: Is it to protect wounding?
V: Understanding is not going to help you; you have to stop it, that's the only thing that works. Understanding it is actually the booby prize.
S: Yeah, I found lately that I have gone into that analytical, trying-to-understand-things, trying to get to the bottom of it, hoping it will go away.
V: It's funny watching people with average IQs try to understand things that even if their IQ was 20 points higher, they still wouldn't understand. It's ridiculous. Stop trying to understand and stop your behaviour, stop being a victim. Stop it. Anything else?
S: No, thank you.

~

S: I turned myself into a victim of my partner on Friday. We were having a conversation and I could see a need or a pressure on me, and in that moment, I didn't see that I made myself feel so I blamed her and then tried to get her to change.
V: Yeah, manipulate and control her.

S: Yeah, it doesn't work.
V: It could work if you had more power, you just don't have enough power, for total domination, which is what you would prefer.
[LAUGHTER]
S: It doesn't work in the way that I move away from my stuff so I don't have to feel it and I don't actually get anywhere because I'm just trying to change everything so that I'm feeling comfortable.
V: Yes.
S: That's not really any way to live. I don't want to live that way.
V: Well, you're doomed to live that way until you die, and so are your brothers, your mum, your dad and everyone you know.
S: So how can I be conscious enough to recognize in that moment that I'm making myself feel and not go to blame?
V: Well you would actually have to find a spiritual teacher who can show you reality and follow his or her instruction to the letter every single time. I took Ken Keyes as my teacher and I followed his instruction to the letter every single time.
S: I've read that book and I get it on an intellectual level, but not an experiential level.
V: No, because you don't get it. You only think you get it. You're dreaming you're getting it. You don't get it. When you get it, it changes your life.
S: There's motivation in me to learn to be able to feel like I'm making myself... I'm causing everything that I am experiencing.
V: What I'm attempting to do tonight is to make you realise how unconscious you are because most human beings think they are very conscious, and this is simply not true. Most human beings are very unconscious, in fact. If you can't stop being a victim, you are not very conscious, you are very low in consciousness as a matter of fact and in making you discontent with that, it may be a motivator to motivate you to become more conscious, otherwise, you are doomed to be a victim until you die. There's the choice.
S: Yeah, I realise it more and more just how unconscious I am and this thing of seeing things retrospectively keeps happening, so it just shows me how unconscious I am at the moment.
V: Yeah.

~

S: I think to myself sometimes that I'm getting better at not being a victim, but I see it running through my day here and there, and I'm not sure if this is right, but it seems to have something to do with...
V: You are constantly a victim, so when you say it's running through the day and yes, all of the time. You jump from one victim-orientated story to another; usually you're a victim of your partner. Pretty much all of the time, and you were given the name you have to remind you to become clear because you aren't and the reason you don't have any clarity is because you are a lousy thinker; you are constantly victim-orientated.
S: Apart from being a habit, has it got something to do with a lack of being able to stand alone?
V: No, stop it. No amount of understanding will help you. People have this stupid idea that if they understand something, it will fix it. It's not going to fix it; understanding is the booby prize – stop it. Anything else?
S: No, thank you.

~

S: I really appreciate the deadliness of the discourse; it feels like there is no room for weaseling out of responsibility. I just see the ways that I was a victim today and I didn't think it was too bad, but then I noticed I got caught so many times. I become a victim of my workers when they don't do things that I asked them to do, and I take action straight away, but it's not from a place of openness and that's mostly because I become a victim. I guess that's all.
V: Okay.

~

S: I think that I saw victim-orientation differently after this discourse today. For example, when I was talking about being reactive with my housemate the other day, I didn't necessarily think I was making myself a victim of that, but I think possibly I was. Would you say that is correct?
V: Of course you were.
S: Based on what's going on there, I am blaming something outside of myself for my discomfort.

V: That's right.
S: When you were 19 and you realised what you were talking about, about victim-orientated thinking, how did you go back through your earlier childhood where you had developed the habit.
V: I didn't, I just refused to be a victim. Being a victim is a choice. Anything else?
S: Did you have to undo the result of the way you were previously thinking?
V: I had to remove some belief systems, but even if I was triggered, I would refuse to be a victim.
S: It's a very good teaching.

~

V: Of course, it would be a very good teaching, why wouldn't it be a very good teaching? Are you complaining? [LAUGHTER]
S: Yeah, because I create my own suffering.
V: I noticed that, you create lots for yourself, you're very creative.
S: At suffering? [LAUGHTER] Yes that's true.
V: You could run a course, "Creative Suffering". [LAUGHTER]
S: I want to create freedom.
V: Oh, well let go. Let go, let go, let go. Anything else?
S: No, thank you.
V: Let go. [LAUGHTER]

~

S: I like the reminder about how unconscious I am.
V: Oh dear! Until we realise that we are unconscious, we're unlikely to do a great deal about becoming conscious. This is why most people never do anything about becoming conscious; they don't realise how unconscious they are. It's not until you come into contact with someone who is really conscious that you realise how far behind you actually are. That happened to me when I came into contact with Osho Rajneesh and I realised I was way, way, way behind, and there was a new mountain to climb; the mountain of higher consciousness.
V: When you said you were very conscious when you were 19, it's just in relation to us?
V: I think it was because I was a martial artist actually and very present. I was more present than anyone I knew, and as a result,

was very intense to be around. People who are present usually are, and that's because they're not dreaming. There are no soft edges around them.

S: I realise I've been quite unclear today.

V: Why do you think that is?

S: I haven't been meditating.

V: Oh, shame on you [LAUGHTER] Must meditate!

S: I've been hanging out with people who aren't very conscious, I feel quite drained.

V: It's not so much draining; it's that they fill you up with certain energies that make you feel tired.

S: Yeah, that's how I felt last week; I wasn't getting involved in any of their stuff.

V: Yes, but energy flows from full to empty, so if you're lighter than others and they are very full and you are hanging out with them, there will be a flow.

S: It seems to happen every day that I am at work.

V: Yeah [LAUGHTER]

~

S: I like the discourse tonight, about victimness, and I like that you've been quite strong on the point of don't try and understand, just stop it, because I notice that I am quite victim-orientated.

V: That would make you unbearable to be around. Victim-orientated people are hard to be around.

S: Yeah, and I definitely notice a tendency in me to try and understand it before I let go and it's like that thing of trying to control it, it's not surrender.

V: No, and in that understanding, you probably try to justify it.

S: Yeah and it's funny because I spent today with my family and I can see how strong it runs in them, my dad is a victim of everything.

V: And that's how he will be until he dies, and he is going to have a very unhappy life until he dies as a result of that, and there isn't really anything you can do about it.

S: Absolutely, yeah, I've tried to tell them, that there is no point, just let it go.

V: They don't want to hear, because they can't hear.

~

S: Today I was down south, and I got to skipper the boat all day.
V: Oh nice.
S: Yeah, it's fast. That was a lot of fun. I love being on the water and I love how present I have to be whilst skippering the boat. I had to be really aware of all the channel markers...
V: ...Everything all the time.
S: ... where all the incoming boats were coming from, the angles they are going, everything. It's just so much fun.
V: People who aren't present shouldn't drive boats.
S: Yeah, for me it's like, whatever story I am in, I just get taken straight out of it.
V: It's a bit like motorbikes. People who can't be present shouldn't ride motorbikes either, because there is no leeway.
S: Yeah, I remember riding a motorbike, especially off-road, and the moment you take your eyes off the trail something bad happens.
V: Oh, not necessarily, could be good. [LAUGHTER] Anything else?
S: No, thank you.

~

S: I liked your discourse. I feel like I'm getting too old not to take responsibility for myself.
V: Yeah, around 40 years ago. [LAUGHTER] Anything else?
S: Yeah, the other gem that I feel comes along with this is you can't give yourself a choice.
V: No, you can't give yourself a choice.
S: Which is the only way out of victimness.
V: It's the only way out, there is no other way because you do choose, it's a choice. As you become more conscious, it's really obvious. The same as it's really obvious that as you become more conscious, selfishness and self-obsession are the enemies of higher consciousness.

~

S: I found myself making myself a victim of the situation this morning. I had a conversation with my partner when I was driving to breakfast and she pointed out that I was being quite negative during the last couple of days.
V: Yes, you were choosing immature roles.

S: Yeah, absolutely and how with the room swap today and being in a role that won't serve me or them, and it was really hard to hear.
V: People who are in victim orientation usually can't hear.
S: Yeah, there was a tiny slither of rationality that kind of crept in...
V: ...the problem with actually owning up to being a victim is it makes you feel like an idiot.
S: Yeah, I did feel like an idiot.
V: Well, you were, and when you own up to it there is a chance other people may see you as an idiot as well so it's best not to own up to it, unless of course you are in the presence of people who aren't victim-orientated and they already think you're an idiot.
S: It was a much better day after that...
V: Oh heck yeah, once you take responsibility the game's over.
S: I was very grateful that my partner was quite gentle in the way she explained it to me because the power of it was quite surprising; the resistance of it.
V: Well it sounds like it was a good insight.
S: I feel like because I have been unwell, and a bit grumpy because of that, it has made it easier for me to fall into this victim space. Are there other things that you've noticed that put people more into that place, or behaviours or actions or habits?
V: I found hepatitis helped, my company manager giving away thousands of dollars of my money when I was sick helped, chronic fatigue for 15 years helped, a few little things, you know?
S: So, you have more victim-orientated thoughts coming through because of those things?
V: No, I refused to be a victim, but it helped me be grumpier. [LAUGHTER] You'll be amazed at how grumpy you can get when your liver is damaged.
S: Maturity is very good.

~

S: Can you be grumpy or moody without being a victim?
V: Yes, you can be grumpy without being a victim.
S: What is that?
V: It's just a mood, it's not a thought pattern.
S: Is it contraction?
V: It doesn't have to be contraction.

S: So, you can be just short and not want to talk?
V: Yeah, human beings go through different moods depending on hormones a lot of the time. Anything else?
S: No, thank you.

~

S: It's a very good teaching. It seems very clear that a successful person wouldn't be victim- orientated.
V: It depends what you consider successful. I consider being happy successful, which rules out most people who are wealthy.
S: A happy person wouldn't be a victim.
V: No. Why would they be a victim?
S: Yeah, I see that at work. I become a victim of the guys getting things wrong and doing what I consider stupid.
V: Yeah, that's why you need consequences. You can train humans similarly to training dogs, for example, with reward and consequence. That's how we were all trained at school actually; a pat on the back or a reprimand. It's pretty primitive, but it works. Anything else?
S: The other night, you mentioned that you didn't think I would hang around.
V: No, because you weren't here for the right reasons when you first came, you were here because you were with your partner, you didn't come for yourself. Your partner came because they were curious; you came because you were with them and so quite often, people who come for the wrong reasons don't stay. You did and I'm really glad you did. Does that answer that?
S: Yes, thank you.

~

S: This is a great topic for me. I think the last victim story I ran was being a victim of myself for being disorganised with the visa.
V: Did you kind of beat yourself up a bit?
S: I did and then I stopped.
V: You activated the internal bully to give you a bit of a bash.
S: Yes, and then I saw how stupid it was.
V: So, then you bashed the bully [LAUGHTER] Right?
S: It makes sense when you say it's not about insight, it's just about practice.

V: Insight is an invitation to practise, yes. Insight is not the answer.
S: Yeah, I used to collect insights.
V: Most people do. Most spiritual seekers collect insights falsely believing that somehow it is going to help them. It usually keeps them in lower consciousness because when a person collects enough insights, they think they are actually spiritually advanced. Now they are totally lost.
S: It's very easy to see victimness in other people, like in my family, it's so obvious. I guess it's less easy to see it in myself because I have an investment in not seeing.
V: Yes, you have an investment in not seeing it, that's true. You have filters. You also have an investment in being right.
S: So, the investment is about not wanting to feel something?
V: It's not conscious; it's just the way you've been patterned. Just stop it; stop being a victim.
S2: You said this is one of the most important subjects.
V: Yes, it is.
S2: When I had my satori when I was younger, I saw this to some degree, and I was like, wow. I obviously lost consciousness and clarity since then. If I'm not happy with life, life circumstances – whatever they may be – it's like I become a victim of how I have created that for myself. It's a weird self-defeating pattern. How do you stop being a victim of yourself?
V: Stop it, yes, that works. Nothing else works, only stopping it works.
S2: So, you saw things in your life that you have failed, and you ruined things and you thought 'okay no…'
V: I didn't necessarily see it that way.
S2: How don't you see it that way?
V: I'm a fatalist, and I have been for most of my life. Whatever has happened is meant to have happened.
S2: So, you don't take long to get to that point when something happens?
V: No, I'm pretty much there.
~

S: I spoke the other day in Satsang about the immaturity I run around my mother and partner; me having "mummy" trips, and today I just noticed, my mother commented on a couple of my photos on Facebook and instantly I am like, just leave me alone, and I realise how childish it is to run that. Normally, I'd just ignore her messages and she would get really insecure and normally, if I respond, I'd write something nice, but I'd be running a "piss off" inside myself, and today I didn't run any of that. I noticed the immaturity and I just liked her comments.

V: I saw that.

S: Yeah there was no need to run negativity, it's just, be pragmatic. I guess I'm just seeing how I treat my partner when my pain is close to the surface and just in hindsight, I don't want to go there again.

V: Well don't.

S: Yeah, it's just not necessary.

V: No, don't do it.

S: Yeah, I'm reading My Mother, My Self by Nancy Friday now as well.

V: Oh good.

S: When I first came along, trying to read that, I just wrote it off because I couldn't understand any of it.

V: It's in English. [LAUGHTER]

S: Yeah, I constantly needed to get a dictionary out to understand a lot of the words and I became a victim of that. [LAUGHTER]

V: Mother(noun): That's who had you. [LAUGHTER]

S: Yeah, I can understand it a lot more now so it's good to read.

~

S: I found your conversation at the very start about how when you got triggered you didn't necessarily lose your consciousness levels a fascinating point because I find that very, very difficult. It seems almost impossible not to go unconscious when I am triggered and that point of you valuing clarity more than anything else or the story of what's going on. The other thing is you are very present and you've always been very present and for me to maintain victimness I have to be, to some degree, living in the past, and there is a break in the dream or in my narrative. It's quite often you going "there's now"... ah... my mind is blown away... sorry I have lost it.

V: Bye-bye. [LAUGHTER]

The Spiritual Ego

V: Welcome to Satsang.

People have identities that they protect, usually because it is who they think they are and quite often it gives them some sense of value. So, a pharmacist who has studied at university has the identity of being a pharmacist; they are quite proud of having spent so many years at university and so many years at school. They make their living out of that, and it's who they think they are to some degree. They may be identified as something else; perhaps if they're involved in sport, they are identified with that as well. It is the identification that is the problem. It is not that they are a pharmacist or a sportsman, it is their identification. In higher consciousness, this identification is the problem. In lower consciousness, it isn't a problem because everybody thinks they are a somebody. Only people who have higher consciousness know for a fact that they are nobodies and live as that. So, people jump into different things and give themselves an identity. Quite often, it gives them an ego boost; it is something they stand behind and have pride in. Of course, it is false pride because it is not really who or what they are. In spirituality, people who meditate quite often have an ego trip around being a meditator. They identify with being a meditator or they identify perhaps with being good at yoga. Or they may identify as being good at self- inquiry, or somehow, they have developed a spiritual ego. These egos are the worst of all. They keep people in lower consciousness because they are very competitive egos.

The idea in higher consciousness is to become less than, not more than, so when I try to take certain things on with people regarding identification, it shows me how stuck they are, and how addicted to lower consciousness they are. This shows up when we're running around trying to boost our spiritual ego somehow because spiritual practice has nothing to do with ego; spiritual ego is simply ownership. It gives you an identity, and if you're good at something, it quite often gives you an "I'm better than you" identity. This has a spiritual pong about it, probably the worst pong of all.

Anyone who has any understanding about higher consciousness knows that it is about eliminating the ego, not about building it up. The new age, and personal growth, is about becoming bigger, better and more powerful. This keeps people in lower consciousness. Higher consciousness is about being less than, always. You look at yourself, and you look at the different ways that you might be hiding behind some form of ego that is giving you credibility. The worst kind of ego is the spiritual ego; perhaps there's no dirtier kind of ego on the planet. Some of the things that are done in the name of Truth are quite revolting.

My teacher Osho was pretty good at taking people apart who had big spiritual egos; he called it the "scratch test". Someone who actually has higher consciousness isn't going to contract inside when you scratch them. He used to take people apart, quite publicly.

In the meditation world, the spiritual ego is not too common in Western Australia, because how can you tell whether someone is a good meditator or not really, unless you read energy, and not that many people read energy. Not many people are that open or have learnt the language of energy.

In the yoga world, the different postures that people can do can be a show of "I'm really wonderful at this, look what I can do, look at me do this pose". This kind of ego is the most dangerous ego of all for the person who has it. It will keep them in lower consciousness, guaranteed. A true practitioner of yoga is a nobody, a nothing; they are not trying to show off. As a teacher, they are simply there to facilitate others in raising their consciousness levels through the practice of yoga. Unless they're just into exercise, which isn't really yoga, that's not what yoga was designed for really, that is just contortion, they should join a circus. If yoga does not bring you to silence and stillness, it is not being practised correctly, no matter how good you are at holding an asana. In silence, you are a nobody, and you maintain that "nobody-ness". Now you are on the road to higher consciousness.

There are different types of egos that get in the way in the spiritual game. People start thinking they are advanced in some way, start looking down on others, start thinking that others are somehow less than them. As you go up in consciousness levels you realise we are all one anyway; there's no such thing as less than, there are just some people who don't know who they are, who are lost. If you're truly interested in spirituality, if you are truly interested in higher consciousness, you have a practice of becoming less than, not more than. Anything that gives you an ego boost is not a helper, it's a hindrance. Anything that has you competing with other humans is keeping you in lower consciousness, not taking you towards higher consciousness.

Twenty or 30 years ago, I used to be able to sit in a full lotus position for quite a long time, half-lotus for hours, thinking that was really good until the realization that I was actually looking at myself through the eyes of others, and how dirty that was. The interest was in higher consciousness. Not just being seen as having higher consciousness, but the real deal. Hence, the practice of openness. Nobody knows what you're doing. Nobody knows you're finding the resistances inside yourself and opening them or removing the belief systems that support contraction. It is all really done anonymously: you can't pin something on your chest and say, "Hey, I've been practising openness. Look how good I am." You don't become "bigger than Ben Hur" because you can do certain postures, you just become open. In that openness, you become less than, not more than, because it erodes the ego, it leaves you with nothing eventually. This is because the ego is a resistance itself. In openness, the ego is gone. So my people are watched very closely to see what they are doing, to see what they are really up to because the interest here is in people who want to raise their consciousness levels, who want to flower as human consciousness. That means removing any obstacle that might be in the way. The spiritual ego is very much in the way: it will keep people in lower consciousness, and it is ugly.

The object of the game is to become a nobody, which is what you really are, not a somebody. Nobodies don't have to prove anything to anyone. There is no effort whatsoever to be a nobody, there is always tremendous effort to be a somebody, especially somebody who is good at something. This game is about effortlessness, about resting in Beingness without any effort whatsoever. It is all about becoming a nobody, and then you can find yourself as reality because there won't be a somebody in the way anymore.

Any questions, any statements, any challenges to this teaching this evening?

~

S: So, with changing patterns, you have to do something different for a number of years, in order to change…these identities, these ego boosting things, do you have to see it or…?

V: Seeing it is pretty good. Like it was okay to sit in a half-lotus for hours on end, as long as it wasn't done in front of anyone else; getting an ego trip out of it by doing it in front of other people. The "look how wonderful he is" thing is ridiculous really. Contortionists could train themselves to sit in a full lotus posture if they practised often enough. It depends if you are into higher consciousness or not. I saw it as an obstacle in the way, and it was.

S: So, what is required to not be an ego, to not be special?

V: Death of the "I". Then it doesn't matter how people see you. Sometimes, people ask why I don't have a problem not being accepted. The answer is there is no one here who cares, not really. What you think of me is your business, I don't care. If you think of me as anything, I don't mind. You take away your identity as what you do for a living and see what is left! You take away your identity as a man, or a woman, and see what's left; because these aren't you either. Some people get caught in thinking they are academics – what an ego trip that is.

S: When I first came here, I was outraged that it was suggested I could be a cleaner for a living because I had such an identity around being a high paid office worker or something [LAUGHTER]

~

V: I recognised this was a problem when I was a publisher. It was very hard not to be a someone because everybody wanted to be me, so I gave everything up to become a true nobody; gave all my money up, all my power up, all my prestige up to be a nobody. The interest was in higher consciousness and no longer in being a big somebody.

S: Lately, you have been pointing out my ego around my graphic design and I notice over the years there are different identities you have pointed out.
V: Yes, and you hang on to that identity so strongly it is very hard to talk to you, you think the identities are real, they are not who you really are. If you haven't studied the psychology of advertising, it won't be advertising; pretty is not advertising. It is about what happens in a person's mind when you present something.
S: I wonder what it is that I am getting rid of when these identities go.
V: Well, identity is dream, it is compacted dream. You repeat it over and over again until it has become kind of solid. It's like a piece of clothing that is stuck on you that you can't get off, a bit like a tattoo. Anything that you've reinforced is going to take a while to erode.

Anyone who has got a strong identity is going to keep themselves in lower consciousness, guaranteed.
S: What about receiving compliments?
V: You should deal with compliments exactly the same way you deal with criticism: it's okay, it's okay for people to see you that way, it's okay, it's okay. It's okay for people to like what you do, it's okay for people to not like what you do. It's okay.

~

S: So, with those women's magazines…?
V: They all have hooks in them, usually to make you feel dissatisfied. They are basically designed by people who have a very good understanding of psychology. They know how to make people discontent.
S: Is it possible to be happy and buoyant in an environment that has a lot of suffering around?
V: Absolutely. It is possible to be happy and buoyant in any environment. All you have to do is be in acceptance of everything. People who are in acceptance of life are happy people. People who are miserable are not in acceptance of life as it is.
S: Recently, when I've been with you and we're talking and there is agreement, there is like an uptick in me or this feeling of acceptance that comes up. Is that where my identity is getting reinforced?

V: Probably, but not necessarily. It depends on what you're getting out of it. Look inside and see: what makes your ego stronger, what makes it diminish? People who have gotten very defensive of their ego are usually stuck in lower consciousness at that point because someone who has higher consciousness doesn't protect the ego at all. They don't have an interest in its protection.

~

S: Hi, is there a link between lack of self-nourishment and strength of egoistic identity?

V: No, people can have the very strong identity of being a loser. They can put a lot of energy into being the loser. It takes no energy to be a nobody; it does take a lot of energy, however, to think you are a loser and keep that going. Look at how much energy people put into suffering. Usually, if someone is suffering, they are identified as being that suffering. That's their identity: "I'm the one who suffers."

S: You said something about being in the full lotus position and how you realised you were seeing yourself through other people's eyes and that there was something wrong with that?

V: Yes, I was into yoga and proud of my ability to sit in the full lotus position. It was an ego trip; people were competing and I was really into higher consciousness, not to be seen by others as wonderful, and I was missing that reason. Here's the thing: if you are competing and you win at something, someone else loses. If you're better than, there's got to be someone less than.

S: How do you go beyond competing?

V: You make everyone win. Everybody you meet, you help them win. Now you are being beautiful. If there are people losing in what you are doing, then there is something ugly in what you are doing.

S: I feel a need to prove myself regularly. Can that go away with discipline, or does it need to be self-love or something?

V: It is about self-love, which begins with self-acceptance. It always comes back to that. People who constantly have to be better than, have a lot of low self-worth that they're defending. People who are better than, are just better than – they don't need to prove it. They don't get anything from it, they are just better than. If you want to compete, compete to see who can be the biggest nobody. In spiritual circles you do get that, don't you worry. "No, I am more of a nobody than you!" [LAUGHTER] I've actually walked out of groups where that sort of thing goes on.

S: I had a satori on a spiritual retreat when I was younger, then later in that night, someone who had heard me talk about the satori walked past me and said, "We're the lucky ones!" Listening to that made me feel sick [LAUGHTER] So yeah, it can get really bad, we don't get much of that spiritual ego in this room with you.

V: Yes, back when I was still a seeker, they tried to stop me from sitting in the front row of Satsang. All the locals occupied the front rows, but one guy arrived late so I got his chair, and the lot of them stewed for that whole Satsang.

S: I admire the quality you have of not caring that a room full of people are upset with you, and you still enjoy yourself, you don't mind. So, what's the best way to diminish whatever ego is there, particularly the spiritual ego?

V: Put Truth first. It will destroy you. There is no room left for the ego if you put Truth first; what's left of the ego becomes a servant of Truth, and in that it becomes devotional to Truth.

~

S: I really like what you said about putting Truth first.

V: Yes, most of the time most people put their ego first. Some people don't. You can tell, when pressure is applied, when things are going really badly, the person who still puts Truth first is a spiritual seeker. That person will wake up.

S: I feel a lot of meaninglessness in my life lately.

V: Well that's accurate. If you examine it, they (this doesn't relate to the seeker's comment. Is it meanings that are only belief systems?) are only belief systems that have no substance in reality.

S: I can see I look for security and reference points for who I am and what I'm doing in logic.

V: Yes, the reference points all go away, none of them are real because they are all ultimately false. Without a thought, who are you? Without a thought, who or what are you? The truth is, it can't be answered.

S: I find my memory isn't so good, what could be happening?

V: Well, one of the reasons memory works is by repeating things over and over again to ourselves so we hold ourselves in a mind pattern. What do you think would happen if you stayed in no mind, or silence, all day long? Well, it doesn't collapse, but it doesn't hold those memories like it used to when it was repeating them constantly.

S: There has been this insight that I am just okay, and I can hold myself in tenderness, even if I show up as stupid or foolish, but lately it has been difficult.

V: You have deluded yourself that it is easy to be okay. Look, you have been giving yourself a hard time. It is in your energy field. You have been sitting in a raft of buoyancy; I don't think you have been using tender okay-ness at all.

S: Yeah, that feels about right.

~

S: Are the different forms my ego takes just an avoidance of low self-worth?

V: They give people a sense of better than; we are taught so much to compete at school. I mean, who wants to be a nobody? Everyone goes to school and gets trained to be somebody and if people don't make it, they have failed, it is all rubbish. Why do you think people have midlife crises? They've been successful, they have gotten everything, and then they realise that it's bulldust, otherwise, they wouldn't have a crisis. It is all a con.

We are actually all nobodies.

Thank you for Satsang, it is good to see all you brave hearts here tonight.

Unconditional Surrender

V: Welcome to Satsang. Are there any questions, statements or challenges here today?

S: I don't understand why I keep on insisting on being real if it keeps me so miserable. I can see how miserable it is, yet it's like I insist. Why would I insist if I can see it makes me miserable?

V: Because you're too unconscious not to.

S: How can I keep the feeling of being more open and vulnerable then, Vishrant? What am I putting in the way of that?

V: You're unwilling to feel pain, so you close yourself down, so you don't feel it. If you became willing to feel the pain that's inside of you, you wouldn't have a problem. Your defensiveness is related to your willingness to feel pain. When you're willing to meet pain, there is no need to close. Anything more?

S: No, thank you.

~

S: Today I went back to work, in a school, and I found it very energetically jarring to be there. It was very intense to be around the staff and children, with the amount of force used in the room. How did you deal with energy because I know that you would work in deep tissue massage and primal therapy. What was your way of remaining clear and effective in that environment?

V: It's not like the energy didn't enter me, but after being a meditator for so long, my mind's awareness can cut through anything, it's so disciplined. It's not like energy doesn't hurt me; it does, but I love clarity, so I don't entertain story. Nothing can sway my mind because it has been trained to stay still. I've been a mystic my whole life.

S: Did you still find yourself holding back and withdrawing from dense energy in that sort of setting?

V: Not really. It's difficult to stay awake when watching a movie with lots of people in the room, so I just go to sleep. Withdrawing is not what I usually do. Quite often, I move closer to people who are angry.

S: So, what facilitated that in you before enlightenment?

V: I wanted to be able to diagnose people as a naturopath and psychotherapist so I opened my energy body and myself up so I could diagnose them and treat them. I found that any form of defensiveness stopped that process.

S: With diagnosing people, was it an energetic sensation? Or was it inner knowing?

V: No, it's energetic. Everyone is transmitting all the time.

S: So, does someone's energy body let you know what is physically wrong with them as well?

V: Well, they can't hide their energy, most people can't. It tells you the truth because most people don't know they're being read. Most people are energy insensitive. They don't realise others have that facility.

S: So, all the information in their energy field can tell you about their physical condition?

V: Yeah, physical condition and mental condition.

S: I just noticed how I still want some form of excitement or intensity in my life. I can see in my slowing down that I'm still looking for something.

V: You are addicted to experience; you're an experience junkie, like many people, like many seekers. That's one reason why seekers don't wake up because Beingness isn't an experience. It's what experiences appear in, but it isn't an experience, so the addictive mind that chases experience won't chase Beingness because it's silent and still. Anything else?

S: What allowed you to find this because you had an incredibly busy life?

V: Incredibly, yeah.

S: Was it any single thing?

V: No, it was learning the answer, the answer is surrender.

S: You didn't really stop?

V: No, but I practised openness, which is the practice of surrender.

S: So, you're okay whether something is happening or not?

V: Yes, I'm okay. In surrender, unconditional surrender, there is an absence of you. There's no one there to be okay with whether things are happening or not.

S: I'm still wanting to entertain myself.

V: Yes, it's just an addiction, that's all. Probably the last addiction for most people to let go of; the wanting to be entertained. So, that's why people who are quite high in consciousness start looking into the experiences of different dimensions because they have access to them, but it's just more entertainment, just more entertainment for the addiction. They never wake up because they become addicted to the realms...

You haven't grasped how important it is to wake up. You think you have all the time in the world. You do not, you don't realise it. The only thing worth doing here is to wake up and when you're in the presence of someone who's enlightened, your chances are relatively high; you think it's going to last forever, you think that somehow you're going to be taken there. That's not going to happen; the people who wake up are very enthusiastic. They will die for truth. They will do anything for truth. They will do anything for heart. That's why they wake up. You haven't realised what's here and how valuable that is. It's a doorway to your own true nature and as far as I know, it's the only doorway in Perth. You get caught in thinking that other things are more important. You lose sight of what's important. Waking up is the only thing that's important. You're not alone; most human beings don't realise the importance.

S: The willingness to let go and find your own true nature, does that come from the heart or the mind?

V: The mind; the heart doesn't do anything. The heart is facilitated by the openness of the mind. It is only the mind that does things, not the heart. The heart just loves, which is not really a doing.

S: You speak about having a love affair with things or being devoted to things. Is that still the mind?

V: Yes.

S: So, what is devotion to the mind... just openness?

V: It is an unconditional surrender if it is true devotion.

~

S: I notice when my partner is busy, cooking, working or doing something, I get uncomfortable, I feel like I'm getting in the way and I want to leave.

V: You're feeling uncomfortable and so you're leaving and running away. You'd need to examine your mind and see if it's all true or see if you're just making it up. You'd need to become more conscious of your mind. Otherwise, nothing can be done. Ignorance doesn't help. The possibility is to have a look and see what's happening inside yourself and see what is actually true or made up.

~

S: Earlier you said waking up is the only thing that's important, and that people get caught in thinking other things are more important and put it off for later. I think that applies to me, so I want to do something differently.
V: And what would that be?
S: To take advantage of what's here with you.
V: Yeah, well if I was you, I would. People who play it safe don't do very well in the game of higher consciousness. They end up watching other people grow.

~

S: I feel very quiet and peaceful in this room tonight. How can I find this space when I'm meditating by myself?
V: It's very quiet and peaceful in the room every night. It's very quiet and peaceful all the time actually. The only thing that is noisy is your mind, and that's not who you are. It's not about finding peace outside of you. It's about finding peace inside of you. If you only look for peace outside of you, you'll become very trippy or easily triggered by people. You have to find the peace within.
S: How do I find that peace?
V: Meditation. I'm not going to teach a different answer. Do you know what my teacher Osho taught?
S: Meditation?
V: Ah yes, that's it. Do you know that is what every other wise teacher on the planet teaches? [LAUGHTER]

~

V: When we betray people, we betray our own hearts, and as you become more conscious you see that clearly. You actually hurt yourself, and I don't think there is any greater pain than the recognition of the betrayal of your own heart. As people open up further and further, they get to see what is there and if they're honest with themselves, they get to take full responsibility for it.

In that responsibility, it breaks your heart open. That you've been involved with something that hurts other humans, this is what happens in higher consciousness. It's why ahimsa exists, because those who are very conscious know this to be true.

~

S: I'm finding that pretty much every day when I wake up, it's like I don't even think of anything. I'm up really early, but there's just pain. It feels like heart pain, low self-worth and anxiety. It's like the first half of the day I don't feel well, then it gets better by the afternoon and there's nothing at night. When I wake up in the morning, it's all there again. So, why is that occurring?

V: Because during the day your defence systems against feeling are being put into place more strongly, so at the end of the day there's not much there being felt. Then you go to sleep and you go into deep sleep and your defence systems relax and you wake up with the pain again. The pain that was always there

S: Is it old pain?

V: Some of it.

S: I haven't recalled any time in my life where I've woken up feeling pain.

V: You've been too closed, you've been too defended. You've been opening up, and in that openness, you're feeling what was there, you're feeling what has been inside you this whole time, what you've been running away from your whole life. You're more open in the mornings than you are in the afternoons. This is what you've created and now you're experiencing it. We're all responsible for ourselves; we're all responsible for our reality in one way or another. If you don't want to feel pain, close up again. Become defended again, become callused again.

S: So, throughout the day, when I become more defended, does that happen unconsciously?

V: It does.

S: So how do I stop putting up the defences?

V: It's the same answer I gave earlier; you have to become more conscious. You're not conscious enough to do that. You may think you're conscious, but the truth is you're not. If you were conscious, you wouldn't put the defences up in the first place, let alone unconsciously. This game is about consciousness, about becoming more and more conscious. Openness facilitates consciousness to a large degree, as closure facilitates unconsciousness to a large degree. You're in a buddha field that opens people. Your best chance of getting free is to be open. Closure doesn't facilitate higher consciousness, it facilitates lower consciousness.

~

S: I've had a lot of feedback in the past about my lack of expression.
V: [LAUGHTER] Sorry, you said that with such passion.
S: [LAUGHTER] I just don't get where... you talk about being with what's happening inside and not what's happening outside. At the same time, it gets pointed out that it's defensive.
V: Yes, it's a defensive role.
S: And all I see is that it's a way I try, I guess, to manipulate how people interact or don't interact with me.
V: I think that it's unconscious, that it's a pattern that you have and it's default now. At some point, you started putting this particular role on and it felt safe, so you kept doing it and now it's just a default pattern. Does that make sense?
S: Yes, so I can see that I can force myself to do what feels uncomfortable.
V: I don't know about that. It would be good for you to have more fun because the role you are running is not a fun role. It's a safe role, but it's not conscious, it's just a default pattern. It's the kind of pattern that bankers or accountants often have, because they can't be seen as "out there" because it makes people feel like they can't trust them with their money. Do you know what I mean?
S: Yeah, I just don't seem to have clarity on how to break the role.
V: Well, I've given you a clue – play more. You see, you can't maintain that role while you're playing, it's difficult. You have to be quite serious to play that role.

~

V: Osho used to have his sannyasins do Dynamic and Kundalini meditations every day. If they were in Mystery School, they had to do it. It was compulsory, so people could energetically clear themselves.

You see, when you come around someone who's awake, if you have nothing inside of you, nothing will come out, but if you've brought a backpack full of pain with you, that's what's going to come out. It's nothing to do with the person who's awake, except they're a bit like a vacuum cleaner. You're the one who's brought the pain, and there is finally an opportunity to heal it if that's what you want to do. People love the energy field, but unfortunately, it undoes you, so you can be free. Seekers look for this energy field so they can be free; part of being a seeker is a willingness to meet pain, otherwise you can't heal the pain body. You're constantly running away. It doesn't go away by itself, and because your mind is victim-orientated, there is a pretty good chance you're creating more all the time. When you start arduously clearing, you start becoming quite unwilling to produce any more because you don't want to do any more work in clearing. In wanting to stay pristine, I stopped producing density by not entertaining any victim orientation, or worry, or procrastination because as a seeker, I was into truth, into being free. The pain body has to be experienced to be freed, usually. What makes it really difficult is any resistance to feeling.

S: Right now, it's very, very silent, and I'm feeling just peace, then I go to work and it's not.

V: There's a book by Jack Kornfield, called After the Ecstasy the Laundry. It's well worth reading. It's a book about people who have woken up. You get the ecstasy first and then you have to do the laundry, which is the work, which involves clearing everything out, and this is the story for anyone who is awake. Jack Kornfield went and interviewed a whole pile of people who were awake, and it's the same story. People think somehow you magically wake up and you don't do any work. Well, that's a lie. There is awakening itself, which is sudden, the preparation for awakening is a process. If the willingness isn't there, there isn't any chance.

S: With the willingness, often I feel like I have the willingness to feel, encounter things and be taken apart.

V: Forever?

S: That's the thing, in my head I'd say yes, but in my body, I feel a closure or a contraction.

V: Well then, you're not saying yes. You're saying yes at a surface level, but not at another level. John de Ruiter talked about this; he said that all the ducks, conscious and unconscious, have to line up going in the same direction for awakening to occur. If you have an unconscious duck saying no, it is facing the wrong way, and your ducks aren't lined up.

S: How do I change that?

V: You have to become conscious of the unconscious ducks to turn them around and say yes, to have willingness; a willingness to be annihilated actually, as an I. The false gets annihilated, leaving it much easier for the real to be recognised.

S: Do you see where my "no" is?

V: You haven't suffered enough. If you suffer more, there will be a part of you that would say; I don't want to do this anymore, and you'll work out an answer. I can give you the answer, but you're not ready for the answer. The answer is simple, it's unconditional surrender, but you're not ready yet. You still think there's another way somehow and there is not. Some people call it non-resistance, which is similar, the same actually.

~

S: You put your hand on my back yesterday briefly and to me, it feels like someone shining a spotlight through me, I feel the discomfort and jaggedness of the energy of non-acceptance of myself where your hand was.

V: Yes, the high-frequency energy is creating a burning as it tries to flow through channels that are closed. You remember earlier when I mentioned that people need to have more fun? If you take away the physical body, we all have an energy body that has channels running through it, and it has different frequencies through it. The whole body has to become high frequency, but most people have rajasic and tamasic energies that are locked in and channels that are half open and half closed. It's a problem, and it's all related to how you think because it's how you think that creates closures and the openness in our energy flow. So, when I put my hand on you, I'm running very high frequency energy through you. It has the potential of blowing you open. That's why I touch people because

I know the frequency I'm running through them has the potential to maybe change something. The Tibetan Buddhist monks are very much into this energy stuff, and it does work to some degree. It usually accelerates the process of undoing, if a person's willing. The problem happens when they go into resistance to what comes up. It doesn't work because it'll bring everything up. When I touch someone, it will bring everything up. It's just a matter of time. That's what happened to an old student, because I was letting them touch my feet, and the feet are stronger than anywhere really. Anything else?

S: When you go around and touch people, you selectively go and touch certain people. Why is that?

V: Because I do. [LAUGHTER] Some people won't be able to handle the touch, so they are not touched. Too much will come out too fast for them. You inject high-frequency energy into a pain body, it's going to come up very rapidly and higher consciousness is about higher frequency. I sent some of you an article on light workers, which is mostly rubbish because most people who consider themselves light workers are not light workers. Someone who's awake is a light worker because light is high-frequency energy. They're playing with high-frequency energy and that high-frequency energy has the potential to help people; if they're not willing, they're not willing. If you have a pain body coming up, it hurts no matter what, and the problem with pain body is you never know how much is there. You never know how much you're carrying. Asanas (yoga postures) are supposed to release pain body if they're done correctly. I did a lot of yoga to open up channels and I did a great deal of acupuncture for the same reason, but unless the mind matches it, the mind closes it all up again anyway. It's all related to how you think, consciously and unconsciously. So, what supports higher consciousness is an open mind, really.

S: Can you open your channels by just opening your mind?

V: Maybe, maybe not. I'm not sure of that. If you hold your fist like a fist for long enough, even if you want to open it, you can't open it. So, things like asanas actually allow the fist to be opened, you see, physically.

S: Can you tell if someone is actually healing themselves or just creating more resistance?
V: Well, healing is just letting go of the pain body really. If they're producing more of it, they're producing more of it. How we think creates the pain body. Our resistance to feeling it keeps it locked in.

~

S: It was pointed out to me that I'm self-judging.
V: How did they pick that up?
S: Ah, I was talking about getting stressed out at work and how I can kind of catch myself being stressed and let go. I must have said something like, "that's just something I do…" along those lines? I'm not 100 per cent sure.
V: It's interesting when people are showing other people their negative side, like the side that beats itself up. It's a defence system. If you're seen to be beating yourself up when you're getting it wrong, maybe they won't beat you up when you get it wrong, and so, the self-critic comes out in a public way, so you're seen as being harder on yourself, which takes away the potential of someone else, in your case maybe your father, being hard on you.

~

V: That book by Jack Kornfield, After the Ecstasy the Laundry, is a good book to read. It actually lets you know that you're not on the wrong track, it's the right track. It lets you know this is what happens to seekers. Carl Jung is a good read too; he talks about it extensively as well. Often, people are unsure. They think they're going the wrong way, but this is just how it is for seekers. They have to go through the "dark night" of their soul. They have to empty out their pain body. When there is nothing left, there is nothing left.

~

S: When you came in, breathing was like ecstasy.
V: Yes, you were experiencing ecstasy? When I walked in, I was also. I walked in and sat down and there was a movement to speak to you all, but there was just such ecstasy. The ecstasy was too strong.
S: It felt like this at the meditation class at Restful Waters today.
V: Restful Waters has a buddha field, so you're meditating in a buddha field. It's very peaceful there because there are no people

there to stir up the energy. Nature has a way of cleansing energy, and there is a lot of nature there.
S: It blows me away that we have this centre.
V: That's why it's so frenetic in the city. If you're energy sensitive and you feel the city, it's very frenetic. Everyone is racing around trying to be efficient.

Conscious Business

S1: I had a business mentoring meeting this afternoon and it was pointed out to me that I need to remain the boss, stay in a position of power and not give my power away to my employees. I said to him that I feel like I sell out with one of my employees constantly being late and not doing things he is supposed to because I feel guilt around him having a family. You and my business mentor both said the same thing: "Be the boss, care, but maintain the power and don't try and be the employees' friend." But I still consistently sell out. How do I hear the advice that's been given and not keep making the same mistake?
V: Well, you can't hear it because you still have an investment in being liked. I have no investment in being liked, neither does your mentor.
S1: So, how do I stop wanting to be liked?
V: Well if you don't love yourself, if you've got low self-worth, it's going to be a little bit difficult because you're probably going to get your value from getting other people to accept you or like you. When you're self-nourishing, you don't need to do that anymore. You can also not need to do it when you see the point actually.
S1: So, just removing wanting to be liked?
V: Well that's a good place to start, isn't it? What do you do to be liked? Are you prepared to sell out to be liked, on what you know is the right thing to do, the right way to be in the world? Are you willing to twist yourself into a knot to get other people's approval?
S1: Yes.
V: Well, there you go, that's your investment. You're never going to be the boss really.
S2: You mentioned parenting the other day; to be a parent first; friend too, but parent first. With your employees when you ran businesses, were you their boss as well as their friend?
V: Always the boss. How can you not be the boss if you're the boss?
S2: Yes, but with your staff, were you also their friend or were you only their boss?
V: Always stood alone.

S2: So, you didn't need their...
V: Couldn't afford to be seen as giving favouritism to anyone; it would have caused jealousy, resentment and bitterness inside the company.
S2: Does that happen in any company where the boss favours one employee over another?
V: Can do, check it out for yourself. How do you feel when you're equal with someone and a peer is getting more favours than you yet you're doing the same amount of work? How would you feel about that?
S2: Yeah, if that was happening, I would get caught. I'm just curious how to be with staff now we have more employees in our business.
V: Well, if your staff lose respect for you, they'll do you in, won't they?
S2: Did you lose respect for being friendly?
V: Who, me? [LAUGHTER]
S2: Would you be losing respect if you were trying to be like a friend to them?
V: I have always been friendly with everybody. Loving people, but standing alone, leaning on no one. I am a man, not a boy, a man. Men can stand alone.
S3: I know that (S1's) mentor is the boss, not a friend, but I've heard him say that if his employees are in trouble, he goes out of his way to try to help them. Is that a part of being a boss? Not being a friend as such but...
V: Being a leader, you take care of everybody. That's part of being a leader; you're a caretaker of everybody. That's why you're a leader because you have the capacity. People who can't take care of everybody can't be leaders, they don't have the capacity to be leaders. A good leader has to be pretty selfless.
S4: I was in the meeting with my business mentor also today and I've made a few mistakes. I had a staff member quit this morning and I see that it could have been prevented by me being more aware or switched on and I noticed that it touches low self-worth and I feel sick.
V: You can get all the advice in the world from your mentor, but until you switch on, you won't be able to hear him or operate what he is saying anyway. The reason he can do what he does is because

he is switched on, he is not lost in dream. If you're lost in dream, you can't hear him, and you can't follow his advice. People who are lost in dream will always make the same mistakes over and over again until they die. If you want to be successful in business, switch on. If you want to be unsuccessful in business, keep dreaming. I haven't met a successful businessman yet who's not present.

S4: When I feel disturbed, I go into dream and I start worrying and panicking. Is that the dream that fogs you out or are you talking about any dream?

V: Well, it's just another dream isn't it?

S4: So, with my mentor's advice, I've made a decision that I'm just going to follow all of his advice.

V: Well it won't work.

S: Why?

V: Because you're not switched on. You don't get it. He is successful because he is switched on. No amount of advice is going to help you because you're dreaming and as long as you keep dreaming, you're going to fail and you're going to make mistakes. You're going to be too unconscious to see anything that's happening around you, like this employee that you missed, who quit today. You didn't see it coming because you're too unconscious to see it coming. No amount of advice from your mentor is ever going to stop that. People who are really successful are switched on, they're not switched off. You're actually quite switched off; you live in your head. People who live in their heads are actually switched off. They think they're switched on, they think they're smart, but the truth is, anyone who is in the present moment will do them like a dinner in a moment and they won't even see it coming.

S5: It takes a person a long time to become present, so how do businessmen get that present?

V: They become killers. You see, people who live in their head analysing don't make it because they're lost. The reason people analyse constantly is because they're frightened so they spend their life in their head trying to work things out, so they'll be safe or make the right decision. These people fail too because they're switched off. They may think they're doing the right thing by analysing everything, but they're switched off and they're losers. Businessmen are like wild animals; they're switched on. They pretend not to be because that's the part of the game, but they know everything you're doing before you even think they can see you. They're switched on. Getting advice from your mentor is great, but it's not going to help you unless you're switched on because you won't see anything coming and you won't know what happened – switched on people see it coming.

~

S: I know that you mostly only say a small portion of what you can see inside the people who come to see you. Why don't you just say what you can see?
V: Everyone will leave [LAUGHTER] People can't handle the truth. They say they can, but over and over again, people have proven they can't handle the truth.
S: What makes someone ready to hear 100 per cent clear direct feedback without pulling any punches or without sugar-coating it, without omitting anything?
V: I don't really know.
S: Were you always able to receive feedback and take it on board and go from there?
V: Yes, well not so much in school, but after leaving school, yes.
S: Is it perhaps when you went into a professional life, into the business world where you couldn't afford to take things personally?
V: I saw openness as an asset and closure as a liability. People who were closed were seen as losers back when I was a businessman because they were. The game is cool, calm and deadly, and wide open. Then you know that you're playing with wolves. If they're not cool, calm, deadly and open, they're sheep, and from a wolf's perspective, sheep are for shearing.

~

S: You mentioned before how much you tell people what you can see.
V: About 1 per cent, if that.
S: So, I feel like you've been telling me a lot of things about me lately, is that still 1 per cent?

V: Less than.
S: So, if you told me 100 per cent …?
V: You'd run away, and you wouldn't believe me because you tell yourself lies about yourself and you believe those lies, so if I told you the truth, you'd think I was lying. You live in a dream world; it's not real in any way, shape or form. You think it is, but it's not. I don't live there, I live in reality. I realised as a teenager if you were switched on, you can't lose because you don't have very much competition, if any. People who are dreaming aren't competition to people who aren't. The crispness and the clarity that come from being present are amazing.
S: I feel so motivated to become present because it's actually quite uncomfortable to be fuzzy and getting it wrong.
V: Yeah, basically you're running some losing programs that fail you, but only you can change that. Nobody can do that for you. Most people like you don't know that people who are switched on exist because you project onto everyone that they are like you, but if you went into my head, you wouldn't believe what's here: absolutely nothing, just clarity. So, I know what's happening to all these people over here while I'm talking to you, absolute clarity. It's not superhuman, it's just switched on, it's just being present, that's all. Present to reality, that's all.
S: Because I'm dreaming, it's like I can't even fathom it.
V: No, because you're dreaming. Dreamers can't do that; dreamers can't be that present to what's happening around them, it's not possible.
S: So for me to become present, is it enough for me to be so sick of not being present to make that change, to make that happen?
V: Well, you have to realise the difference; most people don't realise the difference. Most people don't realise the value of present moment awareness because they are so used to living in their heads, they think it's the only way they can live. They are so used to analysing everything to death, they think that's the only way to be. They haven't even noticed that the reason they are doing it is because they are shit scared of getting it wrong, that they're actually operating out of fear which is a projection into the future that is also not real, another dream.

S: I was talking to my partner earlier about doing a couple of things in the business to grow and I recognised this fear there because I wanted to make sure it's the right decision first before doing it. If I had clarity, then I would know exactly what to do next, is that how it works?
V: That's right.
S: And that's why there's no need to think about it because that's obviously the path, and the clarity in being present would just lead me that way, I'd just know exactly what to do next.
V: Yes, that is right.

~

S: I'm not sure what Satsang it was, but you mentioned that it was dangerous for you when you were young.
V: Yep.
S: And that there were a few different ways of being with a bully. To kowtow, hide or fight.
V: Yep.
S: You chose to fight.
V: Yep.
S: So, I chose to kowtow or hide, very rarely would I fight, and I saw inside myself I don't think I should be that way, or I don't respect the weakness of kowtowing or hiding in myself. What do I need to see about these aspects to see through them, so I don't have the judgment of it being weak and wrong?
V: You have to accept the coward within.

~

S: I was talking to my partner about some people I know and their timeline of buying a house, marriage, kids and other things like that, then he said, "Wow that's really fast," and I said, "No it's not," and then later I said, "Yes, that's pretty fast, it seems ridiculous."
V: Oh heck man, I was married by 21, divorced by 22, had a house at 21, sold it when I was 22 as well, or 23, took a little bit longer to sell the house.
S: He asked why I disagreed with him first and then agreed with him later, and I said something like I register aggressive resistance coming up to him when I perceive him as slow moving in our relationship.

V: Slow? That's because you have an investment in his answer.
S: Yes, I register that, but then I feel uncomfortable because I feel that instead of being on equal standing with him, I feel less than.
V: Why? Why would you want to be less than? If you want to get married, you ask your partner to marry you, buy yourself an engagement ring and force the issue, and if he says no, then he missed out on a wonderful package, you know? [LAUGHTER] Isn't that how it works? It's no reflection on you if someone doesn't like you, it's their bad taste! True! Not only that, not everyone can like you; some people have been brought up differently and want different things!
S: Yeah, I go to feeling uncomfortable because I feel like he knows that I want something from him, so I feel like I'm on the back foot.
V: If someone doesn't want to marry you and you still want to be with them, why don't you just drop it straight away? Why do you want to suffer? Or if that's not what you want, go find someone who wants to marry you. I don't see any point in suffering here.
S: Why are you okay with that, that whole choice to suffer or not?
V: I'm not into suffering. What's the point? It doesn't change anything, and you know – suffering doesn't make you an attractive object! [LAUGHTER] Also, when we talk about suffering, we're probably talking about being a victim, and I've seen that as unmanly since being a teenager. Better to be a hero. It is pretty hard to see yourself as a hero when you're being a victim. If you want to be a legend in your own mind, you can't be a victim! [LAUGHTER]

~

V: I started healing my wounds quite young because I was willing to feel them. They weren't all healed because some of them weren't seen. I made the huge mistake of thinking forgiveness was healing them and it's not.
S: With the low self-worth, it seems like a bizarre thing to just heal at a young age.
V: Well, you've got to learn to like yourself and accept yourself as you are. Having already embraced the darkness in me, it was pretty easy. It's very difficult for people who are unwilling to embrace the darkness inside of them because that's probably what they will be

judging. That's probably where the low self-worth is catching them out, where they don't accept themselves.
S: Is that where it's stuck in me, because I'm not accepting the dark side of myself?
V: You're living too much in dream, so you can't even see what to do. You have to get present before you can see. You intellectualise things; you notice I never do that? Can't be bothered; it's a horrible place to live. What is is what is. You make it work or you don't make it work, that works.
S: Simple.
V: Yeah, very simple.

~

S: Earlier I was singing a song that says, "no words to say, just how it feels, to be loved by you, beloved one" and to me, that song is about what it feels like to have a guru who can love unconditionally and to experience your love in that way.
V: When someone loves you in that way, there's nothing that you can do because there's nothing you've got that they want. So that's real love, it's not love based on bargaining.
S: And some of the conversations you've had with me in the past week have been based out of unconditional love for me and you've been pushing me to look at things and decisions that I've made and mistakes I've made.
V: I have indeed.
S: And to look at my life and what I want in my life. You do that out of love.
V: Yes.
S: I'm reading a book and it talks about love being action, a way you behave.
V: That's not true, not really. No, love doesn't actually do anything. The mind does action when it's affected by love, but love itself doesn't do anything, it just loves.
S: I think it's just trying to draw the difference between need and what people think is love.
V: Oh, well that's not love, no.
S: And true love, which I guess is true care.

V: True love doesn't go away, it doesn't change because it's not conditional on what people do or don't do.
S: How do I love like the way you do on this journey?
V: Well, you can't want anything for you because that's in the way. Remember hearing about my deal with love? The deal is simple – everything for love and nothing for me – that's the deal. I've been saying that now for 21 years. Very few people can hear me, but that's the deal. Everything for love and nothing for me and that deal works. It's a good deal. As a matter of fact, it's the only deal that works, everything else is a scam in comparison because it's a business deal, it's a bargain, it's not love.

~

S: I think you were talking earlier, and you had your cup in your hand and you were doing something energetically,
V: I was.
S: And I was looking at my harmonium and I started falling in love with my harmonium [LAUGHTER] because you were doing something energetically, and it's the weirdest thing.
V: You can put energy into objects and then you can make the objects "glow" with that energy, and when people look at the object it affects them because it's emitting an energy field. That's why when someone who's awake gives food, it's Prasad because it's an energy transfer from the awake person to the food. The food now has an energy form in it that's high frequency. That's why it's called Prasad.
S2: Does the energy put into food… my mind has gone.
V: I just shifted energy with that hand and expanded your mind.

~

S: With what you were saying before about everything for love…
V: …and nothing for you.
S: Yes. In regard to that …
V: You can put up with all sorts of things because you're not expecting anything different. You can put up with hardship, you can put up with disrespect, you can put up with anything because your love isn't conditional on getting any of those things.
S: Something I noticed is when something in my life, for example, business right now, we have an opportunity to…

V: Make a lot of mistakes? To really blow it? [LAUGHTER]
S: Yes, also a chance to succeed. [LAUGHTER]
V: A lot of failure patterns are there that are in the way. You'll do something to sabotage probably.
S: That's what I'm aiming not to do. So, in my mind, when there's an opportunity, I see that I go into hopeful fear, like I go to, "I hope that it will all work out," and a fear that it won't...
V: Leave both out, just make it happen.
S: So, to do that, you just don't entertain either?
V: You just make it happen, don't entertain fear and don't entertain hope. They're both dreams and it will keep you away from clarity.
S: Okay, so did that ever happen to you, like do you ever have hope?
V: I make things happen. There are movers and shakers in the world and then there are dreamers. The movers and shakers make things happen, the dreamers dream about it. Fear and hope are dreams.
S: Thank you.

~

S: I like the talk on being present and being a mover and a shaker. You make things happen in the world, you make it happen, you do it. You become a doer, not a procrastinator. I tend to do all the trivial stuff.
V: Well, if you haven't got someone else to do the trivial stuff and if you haven't got any family to do it for free, you have to do it yourself! Unless you can cultivate some friends who are willing to do it for nothing, this is a possibility. [LAUGHTER]
S: Is it? You did that?
V: Of course! Lots of people will do lots of things for friendship, you know, you help them, they can help you.
S: Yes, that's true. I actually do get a lot of help!

~

S: You said something like true love doesn't have conditions and it doesn't go.
V: Nope, I still love all the people from my past. I love my partner to bits, and she's my best friend in the world. I still love the previous partners who I have had, that hasn't gone, and I still love my son just as I love my daughters, even though he is gone. Most

people confuse love with need. True love just loves. It doesn't have a demand for anything in return, it doesn't go. If it just goes, it probably wasn't love in the first place.
S: Can you get glimpses of unconditional love and still lose it?
V: I first experienced unconditional love when Manisha (first daughter) was born, which was a surprise because I thought I had unconditional love up until that time, and that was when I was 34.
S: So, what is it that facilitates that love?
V: Openness, wide open. It's almost like your heart has an awakening; it's like a flowering of the heart.

~

S: Did you get more present through meditation?
V: No, I got more present because I'm a martial artist. I don't practise, haven't done so for 40 years, but I still know where everyone is around me at any given moment. It's about being present. When you're present, you can see what's happening around you. When you're not present, you're lost. Salesmen are trained to take you out of the moment and into dream. That's what a salesman is trained to do because in dream they can convince you of things that are not real. While you're present, that is not going to happen.

Meditation is like an hour or two hours a day, maybe. Martial arts are all day long. Being present all the time to what's happening around you, all the time. A martial artist is someone who is practising all the time. I was watching a video of Bruce Lee the other day. He was auditioning for a movie. Man, he is the fastest guy I have ever seen. The only way to ever beat him would be to use an Uzi and you'd need a fair bit of distance… actually you wouldn't want to leave your safety on either, by the time you took it off he would have you. [LAUGHTER]

~

V: There's no value in suffering. There's no value in wallowing in what could have been, you know? Everyone here is going to lose a lot because this plane is a plane of tragedy. Everything gets taken off us one way or another, sooner or later and that's sad, but that's how it is, and the more you can accept life as it is, the easier it is. When you don't accept it you really suffer a lot.

S: You just said everyone here is going to lose everything.
V: That's true. There's a lot of tragedy. It's what we are all faced with. Our mums and dads are going to die. They will probably get sick, they might suffer a lot, or they might die suddenly. You're going to die; your children are going to die. Hopefully, they don't die before you. We're all going to lose. We're going to lose financially, we're going to lose in so many different ways. This is the plane we live on and this is what the Buddhists understand: life is dukkha, life is dissatisfying, suffering, because it is. We keep ourselves on a raft and we don't look at that, but it's the truth. Life's pretty much the way life is; it's suffering for a lot of people because they can't handle the loss because they get attached to things and they won't let go of them. Acceptance is being okay with what is, but we're not programmed to move to acceptance. We're actually programmed to move to resistance because that's part of survival.
S: I feel like I'm getting too old to resist.
V: Nah. Is there anything else?
S: No, I'm not too old to resist! [LAUGHTER] No, I'm still resisting.
V: No, you're not too old to resist.

~

S: How much truth can I handle?
V: Out of 100 per cent? 0.001. [LAUGHTER]
S: Why?
V: You're very fragile. Your ego is very fragile. Anyone says anything near the truth to you, you fall apart.
S: Because I don't accept myself?
V: Well, you can't handle the truth. You only want to be told how lovely you are. You don't want to be told the truth. That's why you don't engage me very much because you know I might tell you the truth.
S: How is my ego fragile?
V: I'd say it got weakened by your mother. You weren't taught how to be a man, you were taught to be less than a man. You were kept as a child; you are still being kept as a child by your mother. A parent's job is to teach their young boys how to be men, not to keep them as children.

~

S: I'm going to go to my work tomorrow and hand in my access pass and other things and I'm noting that it's been a security base for me, and I felt mildly sad this afternoon. I'm wondering if it's got something to do with losing security.
V: I'm sure it is. It's not just security, it's also an identity you have and you're losing an identity, so you're losing something. You weighed up a long time ago that that identity wasn't much fun, but you are losing something. That is true, and when we lose things, we feel grief, that's natural.
S: So, if I feel grief, can that be other grief too?
V: Could be, it could be tapping into other grief as well. You don't have to know, you can just allow yourself to feel what's there.
S: You said you could feel my grief a few days ago.
V: Yes, I did.
S: You mentioned it's me leaving my job.
V: That's right because it's a part of your identity, it's a part of your reference points for security and you're losing it, so you're suffering a loss.

~

S: I was very touched by the party last night; I felt a lot of love. Tonight, my housemate made me some dinner because I didn't have time to cook, it just touched me. Why is it painful to feel love?
V: It's not really, unless you're holding yourself away from some wounding, then you open up to feel love and you feel that wounding.

~

S: How do you get ready to hear the whole truth and nothing but the truth? [LAUGHTER]
V: You watch a lot of American television; Judge Judy or something? [LAUGHTER]
S: How do you get ready to hear the truth?
V: Once you get a fair bit of detachment from the mind, it's no longer personal and you start looking at your mind like you're looking at another human being. You just want to see what's real, but as long as it's personal, then you have prejudice, and as long as you have prejudice, you're not going to want to see the truth.

S: That lady you just mentioned, Judge Judy.
V: Yes.
S: Someone was trying to get her to side with being a victim and she just couldn't relate to the concept of being a victim. She was just like, "I don't know what your problem is, just grow up."
V: Yes, she's pretty on the ball.

~

S: You said before about loving unconditionally, but removing the conditions?
V: You have to remove the mind.
S: You have to remove the mind?
V: Pretty much.
S: And you spoke about doing that by allowing the heart to open further.
V: Really, it's about not wanting anything for you, just about being in absolute service to the other. While we want something for ourselves there's a certain closure, there's resistance. It's sort of a business deal. You could say, if you were a loving person, you're devotional.
S: The talk about all for love and…
V: Nothing for you. It's an annihilator, and at some point, if you become conscious enough, you'll realise it's the only deal in town. There is no other deal that works.

~

S: I've been a bit stuck the last few days.
V: Not really, no. You're quite flowing, you're quite gushy really, I wouldn't say you're stuck. You can say that if you want, but I don't believe you. A few days being stuck isn't correct.
S: I can't think of the word to use, something around neediness.
V: Oh, you've been needy. Needing what though?
S: Neediness in relationship.
V: Oh, wanting some attention. Yeah, that can be hurtful.
S: And it's forgetting about this picture of being there to support the other in what they're looking for.
V: Yeah, I mean it's an opportunity to practise self-nourishing or an opportunity to close down, you know? And most people choose

to close down, but as a seeker, you have got to learn how to self-nourish, not close down. Neediness is there because you're not self-nourishing, so you don't get what you want and close down; you cut off, but that's run-away material.

S: Yes, I wanted to ask about standing alone in openness?

V: Well, standing alone is surrender. So first I learnt how to stand alone in resistance in business. Then I got into higher consciousness and realised that if you want to play higher consciousness, you also have to stand alone, but you can't do it in resistance. You have to do it in surrender, which means you have to be vulnerable. In business, standing alone is in resistance. You don't have to be vulnerable; you can stand alone in force. In higher consciousness, you have to stand alone in surrender.

S: Is it still recognising that you still have a need?

V: Well, if the need is there you recognise it, but whether you kowtow to it or not, that's another story. It's really nice to learn how to love yourself. There are a lot of people who will tell you differently to what I'm saying and that's because they are into psychology and I'm not, I'm into higher consciousness, and that's different to psychology.

S: I feel like in relationships I move into very much lower consciousness.

V: Well that's where people lose their consciousness. That's why Gautama the Buddha said you should become a monk or a nun and become celibate because it's difficult in relationship. It's not impossible, it's just difficult. Relationships can be used for truth, or they can be used for you. Is there anything else?

S: Yes, I have a question, but I don't know if it's more psychology than consciousness.

V: It doesn't matter, go ahead.

S: Is there a difference between neediness and vulnerability?

V: Well, I'm vulnerable, but I'm not needy.

S: So, vulnerability is openness?

V: Yes, openness, being undefended actually. Some people think vulnerability looks like someone weeping and carrying on. They may be vulnerable, but that's not necessarily vulnerability. A baby who's laughing and having a good time is still vulnerable, you know? You want to be careful of what your image of vulnerability is because it could be off. Vulnerability is really just wide open; it doesn't actually have a look.

S: Because I think that in the new age scene it is being…

V: …an emotional cripple.

S: Yes, the capacity to express your emotions.

V: Well, more like a baby who wants bitty! [LAUGHTER] There's a difference between the capacity to express emotion and being an emotional cripple. You need to look more closely at the meaning of the words and phrases you are using.

What is Surrender?

V: It's difficult to teach you guys how to surrender, which is really just how to relax, how to be restful, because you're not willing to give up. If you're not willing to give up resistance to life, surrender can't be taught.

I'll relate a story to you. It's something that came to me today. Tonight, while having a listen and a dance to some 60s and 70s music in the kitchen with a friend, a memory came of being eighteen in the Nedlands Park Hotel. It must have been a Sunday session. The local bikies had got me; they were holding me down and putting cigarette butts out on my arms. I challenged the leader, who was probably about five or six years older than me. It was a bikie gang and he was the leader of the gang. I found out later he was a boilermaker who worked down at Kwinana. He was a big guy, you know, one of these guys who does weights, and I challenged him, "I bet you, if we put a cigarette butt between my arm and your arm, you'd move away first."

He took on the challenge because he thought he was a tough guy and he put a lit cigarette between our arms. The cigarette kept burning, it burnt down, and it got pretty painful. At one point, the thought came, "Stuff this!" and I felt something rise in me. I was looking into his eyes and I realised, this thing that's rising is going to lose this for me. So, in letting it all go, I relaxed completely inside and let the cigarette burn my flesh. I looked into his eyes and I was absolutely relaxed. He was tense, uptight and resisting the pain, and he couldn't last. A cigarette will burn for about 10 minutes without being smoked. He couldn't handle it and he gave up, and that was the end of it. He gave up and the gang left me alone.

That was the first time I remember surrendering unconditionally to pain, not resisting it, but surrendering unconditionally. There was no intention of moving my arm ever, but not through resistance, through surrender. There was no way this guy was going to beat me because I'd surrendered, and you can't beat a surrendered man.

Now, how I knew to surrender, I'm not sure, but I surrendered. There was nothing inside of me that was trying to make a move.

There was nothing inside of me that was resisting the pain of my flesh burning. The scars are still on my left arm where those burns happened because I got burnt badly. How to teach that? How do you teach unconditional surrender? It's possible because I could do it, but how to teach it?

I'm pretty sure I had the same attitude towards the Roman Catholic brothers who used to beat me. There was no amount of pain they were going to be able to inflict that was ever going to control me. I didn't resist the pain.

You can't control someone who can surrender. You can't defeat someone who can surrender; they have become invincible. You can kill them, but you can't defeat them. You can't control them. My first surrender wasn't to emotional pain, it was to physical pain.

It came like a flash while dancing – it must have been the music. It was from that era and reminded me of that particular time; how to teach that, how to teach unconditional surrender? Because that's actually what it looks like, it looks like a non-doing. There was no resistance to the burning of the flesh, there was a non-doing. There was nothing happening – that's surrender. The opposite, of course, is doing something, resisting.

It's just a mind trip; pain is just pain. The thing inside of me that wanted not to have any more was seen clearly as a defeat if it was served, the one who wanted to get out. In surrender, it's not that the pain stops, it's just that there's no resistance to it anymore.

All those people who have ever woken up have surrendered unconditionally. Otherwise, they wouldn't have woken up, and that's the deal.

The Zen monks sit for hours and hours in the same position without moving. If any of you have ever done that, you'll know how painful it is. When I say without moving, I mean not moving even a muscle. That's how I used to sit in meditation. No movement. Any pain that occurred was allowed to be there. It was surrendered to, and the other side of surrender to pain is bliss.

This is the methodology of the Zen monks; they just sit, they don't move. Not allowed to move, it's not allowed that you make yourself comfortable. You surrender to the pain. You think they're sitting there in meditation, but they're actually probably practising surrender. Watching the breath, which is surrendering the mind by abandoning it when it comes up, isn't the only surrender. They're probably practising surrender to the discomfort of not moving and to the different pains that arise in the body because of pressure applied to certain points in the meditation. How do you teach that?

Some of you know my history around Shamanism, the extremes that I went through. It was easy because I was able to surrender. If you can't surrender, you can't do anything. We're so interested in being comfortable that we don't allow the possibility of surrender. We're so busy making ourselves feel okay that surrender can't occur. If it's emotional pain we are feeling, we will find coping mechanisms to avoid it. If it's physical pain we will move, we will find a way to avoid it. That means we're not going to learn surrender, but surrender is the only doorway to higher consciousness.

So, how to teach it? I can talk about it, but I don't notice anyone wanting to practise it. If you've ever spent any time with me, you'll notice that I don't move very much because I've actually surrendered. It wasn't just surrendering once, it's a continuous surrender, which is a continuous non-doing and that is against the survival mechanism that is programmed to avoid pain and chase pleasure.

What is your relationship with discomfort, because if it is not a warm welcoming, you will spend your life avoiding pain, flipping from side to side like a worm on a hot tin roof, rather than just laying down and being okay with it.

I remember the profound peace that was experienced looking into that bikie's eyes, knowing that he had lost, knowing that I would never move. No matter how painful it was, there was not going to be any movement. Not through resistance, but through unconditional surrender to what was.

In the game of higher consciousness, you need to take a look at your relationship with discomfort. The interest was so strong in becoming very present again after losing a certain amount of present moment awareness that I just wore shorts and a T-shirt right through winter, hitchhiking around Australia. The cold kept me alert. I wanted the cold to keep me aware of my body so I could keep my awareness in my body and not go to my mind or to dream.

I walked for four years around Australia without shoes or thongs on because I wanted to feel the earth under my feet. I wanted to be present. I was more present than most people I knew, but I wanted to be even more present.

Some teachers say there's nothing to do, but they've surrendered because, otherwise, they wouldn't be awake. I know how difficult that is to do. I know that they must have the same relationship with discomfort and pain that I do, otherwise, they wouldn't be awake, yet they don't talk about it a great deal.

Everybody wants to be comfortable, so they avoid what can teach them surrender, which is discomfort both emotionally and physically. You don't step away from any amount of physical pain, you don't resist. No amount of emotional pain, you don't step away, you don't resist. If you stay and you stay open, you stay vulnerable; you stay in a state of restfulness. This is surrender. This is the doorway to higher consciousness.

~

S: When you are talking about this, I feel so much restfulness.
V: The talking is coming from that place; that surrendered place. There's a transmission of that energy, of that surrendered place, in the words. The same as when someone is uptight, or stressed, or angry, or sad, they have a transmission with their words as well, and it can be received and felt. It's uncomfortable to be listening to people who are coming from a stressed space, or an angry space, or a depressed space because their carrier wave is painful. The underlying energy is painful. I talk about the ability to lift people. If you're carrying stress, if you're carrying anger, sadness, you can't really lift people; you can only bring them down. When people are coming from fear, there is also a transmission in their voice that is not restful, it's frenetic. It will also bring people down.
S: I do practise with pain or discomfort. I just try to make it okay.
V: What about when your wife says something that upsets you and touches you? What do you do then?
S: I do the same. I try to let it go.
V: Trying doesn't work. Trying is actually a loser's game.
S: That's what I mean. It's like I let go once.

V: No, you let go every time, and you come from that place of let go, which doesn't mean you necessarily have to agree or allow someone to walk over you, but that you're coming from a wide-open, relaxed space, even though you may be in pain.
S: Sounds like in that story of the cigarette, it's like you had let it go and it was just completely gone. I've never experienced that; I let go of stuff and then it keeps rising and I let go of it and it rises again. What did you do differently?
V: I loved the pain. Not wanting to be defeated by pain, I found a way to deal with both physical and emotional pain that worked. I'm really not into losing.

~

S: You said you loved the pain.
V: I found a way to love it, yes. Unless you try that, you're not going to know what I'm talking about. You can't intellectually understand what I'm talking about; it has to be experiential. In the same way, unconditional surrender needs to be experiential before you understand it. There's no way you can comprehend what I'm talking about without your own direct experience.
S: Over the years, when things happened that I would consider impossible to let go of or make okay, in your presence you would take me into what I would call a surrendered space, and then it's like once the hurt was gone, I'd be reset, and I could start fresh.
V: Yes.
S: But I would never have lived like that, or rather I think I still wouldn't be like that if I wasn't in contact with you. How do you create that attitude where you start from zero again no matter what happens?
V: I don't like being stale. When you're carrying the past with you, you are stale. You lose your ability to be spontaneous, you just can't play, and I've never really enjoyed not being able to play because I'm caught in some past event. I'd rather let the past event go so I'm free to play.
S: I experienced one time of being completely okay with physical pain and that was when I was in satori.
V: Well, you're very detached from it when you're in satori.

S: I wonder if looking for Beingness can help to go to the surrendered place.
V: If you have a pattern of avoiding pain that hasn't been challenged, it will continue. I don't avoid pain. As a matter of fact, in the place of avoidance, there is a warm welcoming. This isan attitude in my mind. Not that there is any looking for pain, there is definitely not any looking for pain, but if pain comes, it's okay. It's not just okay, it's warmly okay.
S: How do you get that attitude so deep?
V: People give themselves choices and there's a problem in that. You always take the easiest choice. I don't give myself choices and losing is not really an option. You work out failure patterns and then you remove them. The same failure patterns that will kill you in business will kill you in success, in sports, and in higher consciousness. I was a sportsman. If you don't have a relatively good relationship with pain as a sportsman, you'll be defeated by pain because sooner or later you get hurt playing sports, and if you don't have a good relationship with pain, you'll probably stop.
S: I'm pretty gone.
V: That's pretty good. Gone is good. Falling in love with being gone is good too because then the mind starts to look for it more instead of wanting to analyse life continuously. When you are starting to look for "gone", you're on the highway. People who continue to analyse are still in the meandering back streams. Gone is a good sign.

Relationships

V: Welcome to Satsang. Tonight's talk is about how to make relationships work. It took me a while to work out relationships because I don't think any of us are really trained in how to make a relationship work. Quite often, we just model off what our parents are like or we try to do the opposite to what they're like. There's no real understanding of the psychology behind them.

I found, going into business, that business relationships are a great deal easier after working out while pretty young that whoever has the gold, makes the rules; the gold dealer. If you manage to get the gold, you can do whatever you like, but in personal relationships, particularly for men and women in relationships, it's a little more difficult. It's not who has the gold. If you start using the gold to get the other person to comply, it's only a matter of time before you get a revolt. It took a while because being into business for a long time, my main love was business. It wasn't really relationships. Money wasn't the interest so much, but I was very interested in being successful in what I did, and I found that a fascinating way to live, until I didn't.

At the age of 33, there wasn't a great deal of love in my life. I had an amazing life, but there wasn't a great deal of love in it because there wasn't much interest in love. There wasn't much interest in making relationships work. In a lot of ways, my partnerships with women were largely there so I had someone to accompany me out on social events. Maybe having a little bit of fun or something like that, but it wasn't really a love affair. My love affair was with business and success. At the age of 33 when my life was threatened, I realised that all the money I had, all the success I had, all the objects I owned weren't worth a great deal because I recognised that I didn't have any love. For some reason at that point, I recognised that love was really valuable, and that everything else wasn't. I couldn't take it with me when I died and it wasn't very helpful to me because, at that time, I was about to die.

Then it became a little difficult, having to work out relationships. What I did to work out relationships was to have a look at what I would want in a relationship and how I would want to be treated.

I realised that I'd like to be cherished, I'd like to have a certain amount of loyalty, I'd like to be loved, I'd like to be cared for, and I'd like to have someone to play with, someone to enjoy the adventure with. I realised that everyone is different, we're so different. How do you make it work with someone you might not be getting along with all the time? Because we're so different, we don't always get along with our partners. They have different ideas and concepts about how life should and shouldn't be.

I realised that we also have to pay a price: you have to become a listener, you have to be able to listen to your partner, so your partner is being heard, and you have to listen so deeply that you can understand what will make them happy. What will make them feel cherished, what will make them feel loved, what will make them feel lifted.

I was in a relationship with someone who I wasn't getting along with very well, and I realised I could learn a lot from this relationship. I could learn a lot about surrender and acceptance because this person was being unreasonable, running a lot of emotions, a lot of drama, and I've never been much into drama. To me, it seemed quite irrational a lot of the time, but I found that I could accept it if I really, really wanted to. I could accept, but I had to really, really want to. If all I wanted to do was be right, which was pretty easy because I was more rational, well, I could be right, but at what cost? At what price was my righteousness? It definitely didn't bring me closer to my partner; it didn't bring her closer to me. It didn't facilitate intimacy. In fact, it facilitated separation. I got to be right and separate and that's kind of crazy.

You know, if you really want intimacy and you want love, righteousness is one ingredient that doesn't work well in any relationship. There has to be an acceptance that your partner might get it wrong, acceptance that they might not be able to hear you; that they might not be able to see you, that they might not agree with you, and acceptance that it's okay for them to be that way. It's okay for them to disagree and that when they do, you don't go into contraction and resistance.

There may be parts where you can't make it work because you believe in a thing called fairness, so when they're not being fair you just get righteous with them. That will destroy your relationship pretty quickly. That's my experience.

In not necessarily agreeing, but in holding the other in tenderness and openness, and making them feel like they are heard, you can actually have disagreements without getting caught in resistance involving righteousness. You can continue to flow because the moment we get stuck through resistance, righteousness and contraction, the game is up.

I had a couple of rules for myself in relationships. One was to never ever get angry, for any reason whatsoever. The reason I made that rule for myself is because I'd recognised years before that when we direct anger at another human being, we're actually directing violence towards them, and I don't feel we have a right to be violent to other human beings just because we don't agree with them. So, that was one of the rules I made for myself: no anger. That meant staying open and trying to keep away from blame; trying to keep away from turning myself into a victim of the other because that's how anger gets fuelled, through blame.

The next rule is pretty simple: never abandon, never threaten abandonment. The reason I came up with that one is simple: most people have wounding around abandonment, wounding around being left out, being rejected. If I'm truly in service of love, truly in service of making this relationship work, why would I try to wound the other? Why would I threaten abandonment, which touches their wounding and hurts them? So, these rules I made: no abandoning, no anger. Good rules.

Another rule I made was cherishing. Showing that I was cherishing them, saying the words, showing in actions that little bit of care, that little bit of attention, making the other feel special in your life because I was into love. You want to be into being, right? Well, you're not into love. You're into being right and you'll pay the price for that. Love tends to be facilitated by openness, not by closure.

Nobody really taught me any of these rules; I just worked them out as I was flowering through my third marriage. [LAUGHTER] I never left any of my wives; they all left me, probably because I was too righteous. I still love them all. I can't see any reason not to love someone just because someone leaves you, even if they want to take everything with them, that's still not a good reason not to love them. What is your love based on? Is it based on whether or not you have material objects and whether or not they do certain things?

Love is the most beautiful thing in the world to have, but it demands your openness. It demands your acceptance and sometimes demands you putting yourself in second place rather than first place. I love people; I love people in my life. I love strangers who I meet. I won't put anything in the way because as far as I'm concerned, love is the true jewel of consciousness, and if we're going to serve anything, it's a worthy thing to serve, it's noble. So, in relationship with people, I don't get angry, I don't express violence towards them, I don't abandon them, I hold them, I love them, I cherish them because I can't see anything better to do here on this plane, on this planet. I created this reality – you're going to create yours. You're creating yours now and you've created how you've been up until now. We're responsible for how we are, nobody else creates it, and we do it to ourselves.

If you're a loving, caring, cherishing type of person, that's what you've created. If you're not, that's also what you've created. You're responsible for it, nobody else. If you want to change, you can. It might be difficult, but you can. I recognised that making money for the sake of making money and being successful wasn't very noble. I was looking for something noble. I found serving The Way of the Heart, which is actually the Buddhist way, to be noble. There's a nobility in putting yourself aside for others, in making other people's lives work better, in making them feel loved and cared for. There's nobility in that. I recommend it to all my friends.

Any questions, any statements, any challenges to this teaching this evening?

~

S: Just curious, why do you feel that expressing anger towards someone is doing violence or leaning towards doing violence to someone?

V: It's not leaning towards doing violence, it is violence. The reason I say that is because as I opened myself up more and more to feeling people and feeling things, I felt that when people get angry, they inject others with a certain energy field. Quite often, as the energy goes in, it circulates around them and wants to come out again. It's an irritant, angry energy that comes around. When you get angry with someone, you're injecting them with that energy and it comes back out, then you've got war.

I see that if we're injecting someone with an irritant energy, that's a form of violence. That's why I say that. I didn't recognise that until I became more energy sensitive and I also didn't recognise it because I didn't want to. I don't think we like to think of ourselves as violent people, but just because we don't hit people, it doesn't mean we can't be violent with them, with the way we talk and the energy we put behind those words, particularly if it's the energy of anger. Does that make it clearer?

S: Yes, thank you.

~

S: One of the ingredients that you mentioned in the discourse was around play and making a relationship work. I recognised that I don't play enough in my relationship because I get busy and take life really seriously, and then I forget to play. I just wondered what ways you're referring to with play and how to have more fun and bring play into a relationship?

V: You should come shopping with me. Playing happens with everyone I meet. The only reason adults don't tend to play, unless they're drunk or stoned, is because they're frightened to be seen as less than or foolish. What age were you when you stopped playing? There are seven and a half billion people on this planet and they're all there to play with. Now, they might not know that, so you have to be a little careful, but they're all there to play with. What stops us from playing? Man, I love playing! I play with everyone. You should come out with me one day and watch.

The only thing that stops people from playing is fear. What are people going to do? Tell you that you're a schmuck, tell you that you're a fool, that you're an idiot, reject you? Well, that's already been done, too late!

S: You said that righteousness is one of the things that could really kill a relationship.

V: It's deadly. I'm right and you're wrong.

S: Yes. I have a pattern of selling out for approval and that builds resentment and bitterness inside over time and that seems like the opposite of righteousness. I'm trying to figure out, how do you find a middle ground between not speaking up and speaking out in a way that causes harm?

V: Okay, one of the things with friends is that it's good to be able to tell the truth. I'd really rather not be with people who don't like to hear the truth. My whole adult life, even as a businessman, I surrounded myself with people who were willing to tell me what they could see about me and I had an agreement with them that I could tell them too. In this way, I got to see a great deal about myself because they pointed out things I hadn't seen because I had filters on, so I couldn't see. When we start just telling people all the good stuff and not actually telling them what they're doing that might not be savoury, and we're doing that because we don't want to feel rejected, how good is our friendship really? What kind of friend are we when we're not willing to sacrifice a bit of rejection to tell them the truth that might be hurting or damaging to them? Friends who are willing to tell the truth are valuable.

Fortunately, having never considered myself a good guy, the truth has never hurt too much. People who consider themselves good guys, you know, "White Knights," they can feel quite hurt when they're told the truth about what they're really like. If you really examine your own psyche, you'll find that it has everything in it: the good, the bad and the ugly.

~

S: You were talking earlier about not just vocalizing love and cherishing, but actually showing it, through your words, your actions, your gestures, through the little things. What if, basically, I'm just too frightened to show my heart, to wear my heart on my sleeve and just express the love that I have for another?

V: Is there another place to wear it? [LAUGHTER] There's only one place to wear it and that's on your sleeve. What, have you got it in a cage somewhere hidden inside your chest?

S: Hidden, yeah.

V: Because you're a bit frightened? Well, if you do that, you're going to play life-be-out-of-it, big time. Sure, if you have your heart on your sleeve people are going to hurt you because human beings do, they hurt each other. That's how it is. I tell you, it's the only place to keep your heart because love is the most beautiful thing in the world and it's worth being hurt every now and again for it. Just so it can be out there.

S: That sounds really cool.

V: It's pretty much guaranteed you're going to get hurt if you wear your heart on your sleeve. If you don't want to ever get hurt, lock yourself away somewhere and keep your heart away from everybody. It's best. Of course, it's going to be a miserable old life.

S: Yeah.

~

S: You talked about rules in relationship. Do you have any kind of guidance on how to choose or find a good relationship or choose someone you might be compatible with?

V: In relationship, we have the opportunity to love someone and that is a gift. We don't always get along with our partners, but that is no reason not to love them. When these challenges arise, if anything gets caught in you, in a way life has given you what you need to learn surrender and acceptance. In surrender, you are providing the right ground for love to flow through you.

~

S: How do you go in a relationship when one partner always brings up bad pasts and uses it against you?

V: One of the ways you can get someone to stop bringing up bad events from the past is to agree with it. They're looking for a reaction; they're looking for you to go defensive. The moment you don't go defensive and just say "Yeah, that's what I was like," it's often over. [LAUGHTER]

We're talking about disempowering someone using the negative past on you. Just agree with them! They're looking for a rise, they're looking for resistance. No resistance, no rise. As a matter of fact, almost a celebration, "Yeah, thanks for reminding me, old times are not forgotten." [LAUGHTER]

~

S: You spoke earlier about anger and I just wondered, if say for example I've gotten angry or just said something stupid and upset my partner in some way, I get stuck and then feel kind of clumsy in rectifying and patching up afterwards and how to…?
V: How about an apology? I'm sorry, I shouldn't have done that; I shouldn't have said that, I've made a mistake. How about an apology?
S: Yeah, I think that's where I go, but if I've done it a few times before it just seems like, oh God I've done it again and I don't want the apology to be…
V: …cheapened.
S: Yes.
V: It's a new occasion. You can't step in the same river twice.
S: I like that. [LAUGHTER] that is true.

~

S: So, if I look at my parents and their relationship, I can see that what I've modelled from my mum is someone who uses anger to get her way, as a way of being in her power, and I recognise the destruction that causes, but how to not be a sellout and a pushover without going to anger? How to do that?
V: Well, you don't have to be angry to say no.
S: Yes.
V: You don't have to be angry to say, "I want it this way." There's nothing wrong with being passionate; there's a difference between being passionate and being angry. One of them has a massive contraction in it with blame, and the other doesn't. You can still emphasise your words, but can you emphasise your words without getting angry? We all can because we're all great actors.
S: Yes.

V: Imagine being in a relationship where one partner dominates the other with anger all the time. Where's the intimacy? Where's the beauty? It's ugly and it doesn't need to be that way.
S: I feel like if I am actually going into conversation conscious enough to say, "Okay, in choosing my approach with someone I disagree with, to choose to be passionate, but open, not angry."
V: Great, good. Choose that.
S: However, I find that anger arises as a hair-trigger.
V: Catch it and back it off. Recognise that it's toxic, it's poisonous and it's going to do damage. Back it off. Still maintain your position, but from a place of openness because anger is massive closure, so you back it off. Become reasonable. It can only get fuelled by you being a victim. Existence is doing what it's going to do, your partner is doing what he's going to do. Getting angry isn't going to fix it.
S: So, with a repeated pattern of catching anger when it arises, does it eventually stop arising or is that a separate thing?
V: In my experience, it does, yes. If getting angry is a default pattern in you, it's going to take a fair bit to change.

~

S: I've had a real issue with anger and in learning a lot about anger, I'm recognising that underneath it, there is generally sadness or a hurt that I'm not dealing with. I'm going to anger as a default to avoid feeling and addressing the hurt. So, in slowing down, I find moments where I become conscious and say, "Okay, I actually feel hurt by what may have just been said," and I go to the pain rather than anger. It's often a disempowering space. It feels like there's an inbuilt aversion to being disempowered. How to deal with feeling disempowered?
V: I'd like to know how you're being disempowered.
S: Well, it feels like if I feel that hurt, it's almost like a vulnerable place, and to be that vulnerable in the heat of the moment, then I'm at the mercy of somebody else.
V: Ah. Why don't you allow yourself to be that vulnerable and make that okay? And also make being hurt okay? See, not making it okay is how or why we get angry. Anger is like a defence system; it stops us from feeling our hurt, it stops us from feeling a touch. We empower ourselves with anger, going to blame. We gain a

certain amount of control, a certain amount of power, but at a tremendously high price.

S: High, high price.

V: Because it destroys relationships. If we were just willing to feel what was being touched and allow ourselves to be vulnerable, even when we are in conflict, we can get through it because we're adults, not children. We're adults. You couldn't expect a child to do this, but an adult, yes.

S: Yes. There are moments when I'm running unconsciously and the moment of catching it, sometimes is within a few minutes, sometimes it's 10 minutes, an hour, maybe a day later because I'm lost in the story of it.

V: The victim-orientated story. When I started dealing with my anger, I was a teenager and sometimes it took me days to settle down because I was a very angry young man, but I got better at it. If we really want to change something about ourselves, we can if we really want to, and I'm not talking about repressing anger either. I'm talking about not supporting it, which is different.

S: I can recognise the toxicity that's been in my life because of it. Becoming conscious of it has been a long process. I think it's a hard thing to work with.

V: It was good to get in touch with how we create anger as a teenager and how we can stop it because, by the time I was 24, I was running companies. Being angry with staff members is not an okay thing to do, it's just not okay. It just doesn't work because they end up getting bitter and resentful and want to get you back. You end up with saboteurs.

You actually have to maintain a cool, calm and collected position, and that means not being a victim of them, not turning yourself into a victim, not getting angry. You just make things work. Basically, you're stepping into a more mature way of living.

S: Yeah, for sure. I'd say it's one of the hardest elements of the journey in looking at myself and working with myself. Actually, accepting what's inside of me and not being ashamed about it.

V: You look at the justifications for it and you realise why it takes you so long. People justify their anger, and so why would anything

change if it's being justified? Your responsibility is being mitigated. Yet, we are totally responsible for our anger.
S: And it's like the smoke of the flames of something else, something else going on underneath.
V: It's usually defending us from feeling something uncomfortable; maybe a wound.

~

S: I find… I have trouble…[LAUGHTER]
V: I can see that. [LAUGHTER]
S: …Actually letting love in and so, if I…
V: If you let love in, you could get hurt. I wouldn't do that [LAUGHTER] That's the thing about wearing your heart on your sleeve, you can get hurt. Not being able to let love in is you hiding your heart away somewhere.
S: It's like my mind will negate it or twist it and have negative filters and I'll distance myself. Is it just the fear of getting hurt?
V: It probably developed when you were a child, when you weren't emotionally mature enough to actually deal with the hurt coming your way. As adults, we should be able to deal with that kind of pain, we should be able to be mature enough to deal with that kind of pain. So, we have to look at maturity here, and maturity is about taking full responsibility for ourselves, including that we make ourselves feel. Other people don't make us feel, we make ourselves feel. We're the ones who turn ourselves into victims. A bad thing can happen, but we can make ourselves a victim of it or not, that's a choice.
S: With making yourself feel, when I'm not engaged in any situation, it's very obvious, but I find it hard to have that detachment when I'm involved, and I will go to blame. How to have the maturity to see that?
V: The reason you can't see that is because you're lost in some form of dream. You don't have any detachment from your own mind to see what it's up to, so you're basically in a very unconscious space. So unconscious that you can't see what you're up to. That's why in Buddhism, we recommend meditation and mindfulness because it allows us to develop some separation from our mind, so we can see how it's operating while not getting caught in the story.

I don't think there's any magical way that suddenly you can become more conscious as to why you're lost in dream, I don't think that happens. I think you have to actually work towards higher consciousness. We lost a lot of our consciousness when we went to school because we started dreaming, we started living in our heads, which we didn't do before we went to school. Now that we're dreaming and living in our heads, our levels of consciousness aren't that high, and it's not until we get out of that dream that we start to raise our consciousness levels.

~

S: I find myself in relationship becoming a bit controlling and you were talking about cherishing. I want to work towards that goal instead of constantly demanding my own way. Is it simply seeing what I'm doing and asking, "How can I support you?"
V: You can ask if you like, but you know, usually we know how we can support another human being, especially if they're our partner. You can ask them, "How can I support you?" But they might kind of look at you and go, "What, haven't you been living with me or something?"
S: Sorry I meant to ask, "What would you like to do?" And you go along with what they want to do?
V: If you want to. [LAUGHTER] It's your choice. I just like the company of my partner and I don't really mind what we do because I just like the adventure of being with my partner, you know? But sometimes I'm going to want to do what I want to do, and sometimes she's going to want to do what she wants to do, and that's okay. A lot of the time, I just like being near her, it doesn't matter what we do.
S: That's so beautiful. How can I lift my partner more?
V: Do weightlifting first. [LAUGHTER] Like Arnold Schwarzenegger, building your muscles and then when he comes into the room you can lift him onto his chair.
S: How do I lift my partner to where he wants to go in life?
V: You want to lift them to where they want to go in life? Just support them in what they're doing, if you can. Depends on if you have the skill to or not.

~

S: I think you were talking before about your sleeve being the only place to wear your heart.
S: Yeah. I'm not sure if it's on the left or the right, because it hurts in the middle. [LAUGHTER]
S: If I've been hurt, how to decide that that's the best place to wear it when that's the most dangerous place?
V: I haven't discovered unbearable pain yet. People believe there is such a thing, but I haven't discovered it to be true. We can take it. If we're willing to be with pain, we can be with pain. Heart pain can really hurt, but we can take it and then you just make life work while that's there because if you avoid it, you're likely not to heal whatever wounds have come to the surface. If you are willing to be with it, you can start to heal the wounds of the heart, which may have nothing to do with the current relationship you're in anyway. You may have something you've brought in that's come from your childhood or your past relationships. Our willingness to feel our wounds of the heart is the way we heal the wounds of the heart. As adults, we can handle pain if we want to. It's up to you.
S: I guess I've been working on myself, getting rid of the past.
V: How do you get rid of the past? It's already gone.
S: Accepting the past.
V: Accepting the past, that must mean you're still carrying it.
S: Yes. Anyway, [LAUGHTER] I've taken on your teachings.
V: Oh, that's dangerous.
S: When I go home, my partner will ask me what I have learnt. I wish he would come with me actually. I asked him to come with me, but he seems very...
V: Can I give you some clues. Would you like some clues? Some hints? Some suggestions?
S: Yes.
V: When he says what have you learnt? You say, "I have learnt to love you more."
  [LAUGHTER] I'm telling you what works.
S: I guess it's with other things as well. This is what I've learnt for myself. I find I've been doing a lot of reading, meditation, trying to be in a better place, but if he'll ask me the questions, I'm put

on the spot to explain how I feel. Then he'll always defend himself and try to prove me wrong.

V: Okay, but somehow you're not accepting that's what he's like. What if you were just to accept that that is what he's like?

S: Yeah.

V: The non-acceptance in you is hurting you and it's not changing him.

S: So just accept that he's....

V: Acceptance doesn't mean that you stop trying to explain, it just means you're coming from a place of acceptance rather than a place of non-acceptance. You're coming from a place of openness instead of a place of closure, that's all.

S: Let him have his...

V: The way you put it is not quite what I'm saying. It's about accepting that he is like that. Rather than expecting him in some way to be different than that. Are you getting what I'm trying to say?

S: Hmm...

V: You don't want to. [LAUGHTER] I understand. I teach a lot of people and they do a lot of things I don't like from time to time, to themselves, to others and to my property. [LAUGHTER]

But I am in acceptance of them as they are. That doesn't mean I'm not going to actually talk to them about what they're doing and what they've done, I'm talking to them from a place of openness because I accept them as they are. I accept that they'll probably never change.

This expectation that people will change hurts us; it's based on a belief that they should change, and that belief is a bit out of touch with reality because most people don't change much in their whole lives after the age of 20. You know?

S: Yes. I do accept that he probably won't accept.

V: Take away the word probably. If you want to suffer a great deal, just keep on not accepting. All that will happen is that you will suffer. If I can give you one thing tonight, it's just for you to look at how acceptance will affect your life with your husband for the better, rather than what you've been doing, which hasn't worked; your non-acceptance of him as he is. Okay?

S: Yes.

~

S: I really liked that exchange then. If someone is irrational, do you still state your case or is it better just to listen?
V: Whatever works. Whatever skill level you have to work with, but coming from a place of acceptance or non-contraction rather than a place of closure and defensiveness. Once we've moved to defensiveness, we've moved to war. The first signs of war are defensiveness.
S: Thank you.
S2: When I get offended by my partner and I get flustered, how can I just drop that and come back to zero?
V: The way to do that is to drop it and come back to zero straight away. That works, unless you want to hang on to something, but that's your choice.

~

V: Does someone have their hand up? Hello there.
S: Hi Vishrant. In terms of acceptance, if you realise you're in an abusive relationship, and going back to the non-abandonment rule, can you not just set up a boundary and say, "Okay, I accept that he's going to be like that, but I'm not going to accept that into my life, in my environment."
V: Okay, I don't encourage anyone to accept being abused, you know? If you're in a relationship where you're being abused, you're in the wrong relationship. People don't have a right to abuse you, to be violent to you. You deserve way better than that. Does that cover that?
S: Indeed. I guess there are different levels of abuse. Some people probably wouldn't even realise they're in an abusive relationship; it can stem from physical to emotional to behaviours you've learnt as a child. It was just a question because you were talking about acceptance. There's got to be a point with that acceptance where you realise, you're not going to accept that internally so I'm going to move on.
V: The problem with accepting abuse is we're teaching the other that they may continue the abuse. It's a bit like bullying. If we let the bullies bully us without doing anything about it, the bullying

doesn't stop. The bullying only stops when we stand up to the bully, do you know? So, I am talking about acceptance and you can accept they're a bully, but that doesn't mean you need to put up with it. You can say, "No, not going to happen," and you can leave, or they can leave, or you can make arrangements to seek counselling. If you don't do something about it, it will not stop because you're teaching them that they may get away with it again. Does that make sense?

S: Yes, and if you have a rule of non-abandonment, how would you implement that? If you're going to leave them, that's a way of abandonment?

V: Yes, and maybe I should have put a caveat on that. If you're being abused, it's time to leave. That's not abandonment, that's escaping. [LAUGHTER] I'm just playing with words here; no one has the right to abuse you. You do have a right to be loved. How's that?

S: I know. Thank you.

V: Some people have such severe wounding around being abandoned; abandonment wounding, rejection wounding, that they'll put up with all sorts of abuse unfortunately. Unless you stop it, it does not stop, sadly.

~

S: Speaking about abandonment, I think I've heard you speak before about other forms of abandonment within relationship, so not just leaving...

V: Withdrawal of love.

S: Yes, can you speak more about that and how that affects relationships?

V: Sulking is a form of withdrawal of love. Ignoring the other is a withdrawal of love. Not talking to the other is a withdrawal of love and it's a form of punishing the other to try and manipulate and control them in some way. It's not nice, not going to create intimacy, not going to support love. It will create separation, bitterness and resentment, pretty sure. Look and see for yourself and see what happens.

S: Yes.

V: You've got to learn to reach out. Make it work. Make it so.

~

S: You talk about, in relationship, that you can be firm and be passionate and get your point across, but not withdraw love. How do you be firm and passionate, but still be loving with the other?
V: The question answers itself. You just can. If the relationship involves abuse, an ability to connect may be best achieved through mediation from an external source. A counsellor who actually specialises in relationship counselling could be helpful. As a counsellor for 10 years and as a psychotherapist, I saw a great number of people who were in abusive relationships. I did offer couples counselling and basically, taught them what I'm teaching here tonight. How to be with each other in a non-violent, communicative way, and sometimes an outside source is required. Sometimes, if you really want to make it work, you need to get someone to help you.

~

S: Regarding pain, is accepting pain allowing it to be there for as long as it likes?
V: Yes.
S: And a follow-up question. I'm experiencing a lot of heart pain. I find that when I sit to meditate it's the most prominent thing in my awareness.
V: That's really cool. So, if you have heart pain and it's not caused by a heart attack, [LAUGHTER] because if it is, maybe meditating isn't the right thing to be doing, but if it is heart pain caused by some emotional issue, the pain itself is real and meditation is about putting awareness on that which is real. So, if the pain is there and you're keeping awareness on it, you are meditating. Okay?
S: Yes.
S2: Would you also keep the awareness with the breath, or would you...
V: Yeah okay, that's a good question. I used to like to do a thing called Walking in Zen, where I would take a walk down the beach. I used to love walking for miles and miles, or nowadays kilometres and kilometres. What I would do is start watching my breath as I was walking, just watching it here at my lip. Then I'd start being aware of my footfalls as they were hitting the sand and the water

on the edge of the beach. Then I'd become aware of the sun on my body and any wind that might be hitting my face. So, I was aware of my footfalls, my breath, the sun and the wind. Then I became aware of the sound of the waves. I was being aware of five things at once.

Now if you can go into dream and think while you're being aware of five things at once, you'll do better than me. Walking for kilometre after kilometre with everything in my awareness was like an ambient awareness. That is meditation. You don't have to have your awareness on just one thing like the breath to be in meditation. All you have to be doing is having your awareness on something that is real, and the only thing that is not real is what you think. Thoughts are not real.

S: I had a similar experience on my motorbike this week because as I was thinking, I was listening to my thoughts. While doing so, I was shifting and doing all these other things and then I became conscious of that, of those multiple, I guess conscious thoughts about thinking and thoughts about the physical aspects. So, I started to think in my mind, "I'm thinking all these things I'm doing, which I'm doing unconsciously. Am I actually thinking about doing those things?" Like shifting, do I have a millisecond to think about shifting my gears and is that...

V: I don't think so because if you're riding a motorbike and you've ridden it for a while it's all automatic, you're not thinking about it. It all happens by itself, particularly if you're going fast. You can think about it if you want, you can bring your awareness to it and start thinking about it, but most of it is automatic and unconscious. By bringing our awareness to what we're doing, which is called mindfulness, we're becoming aware of our hand movements, we're becoming aware of what's actually happening, rather than what we think is happening. Does that make sense? Or we can think about it, but if we're thinking about it, we're actually still dreaming a little bit and the idea of meditation is to get away from dream and back to reality. The reality is the changing of the gears. You may be using the clutch; you may be using the brake. You're aware of things that are actually happening rather than thinking about things that are actually happening.

I love motorbikes by the way. I had to sell my last motorbike four months ago. It was a beauty, a Triumph 1050 Triple and I could not get it off the back wheel. [LAUGHTER] 125hp and it just flew up the highway on the back wheel constantly and the thought came, "I'm too old for this." So, I sold it.

~

S: Could you please speak a little more on why emotions like pain or love or anything else is real, but thoughts are not.
V: So, pain is real. It's actually happening. What we think about pain is not real. Pain is a sensation that is real. It's actually happening. What we think about it is a thought, it's a dream, it's not really real. It may actually describe what is happening, but it's not what's happening. It's a dream about what's happening. Does that make that clear?

Love is different again. My experience is that love is actually real, it's not a thought. It's actually real and when the heart opens and love is actually experienced, it is the most beautiful thing we as human beings can experience, but it's not created by the mind. It's actually something that is real, it's not a thought.

Now we can think about that, that's thought. The experience of love itself is something that's real. Does that make sense?
S: Yes it does. When I had some life coaching counselling a little while ago, the approach the counsellor talked about was that thoughts create feelings and feelings create actions.
V: They can do, sure. Your thoughts can create misery, can they not? You know we can think ourselves into hell, but we can't think ourselves into love. My experience is that if we're open enough, love comes, and if we're really closed, it doesn't. It seems that there's a relationship between openness and love.
S: So, thoughts can create feelings, but feelings can arise without thoughts?
V: Yes. Some wounding can get touched or it can come up. We can wake up in the morning and we're feeling something, then our mind can put thoughts to what that feeling is about because our mind wants to control it. It doesn't want to feel that uncomfortable feeling, so it creates a thought, "Ah that's because such and such

did such and such to me the other day." And the truth is that's not what happened at all, just some old stuff has come up.

S: Yes, I just woke up with a feeling and started thinking about it.

V: You've got to be careful with those feelings coming up, that we don't start blaming the person closest to us.

Okay guys, thank you for Satsang. Good to see you brave hearts here tonight. Good questions, thank you.

Sangha – Jewel of Consciousness

V: Welcome to Satsang. One of the reasons that the Sangha was created was because people who are going through the process of the dark night of the soul, which occurs as you undo and strip down the ego, need support, and if they go to a normal psychologist or counsellor out there, they're likely to get coping mechanisms to put themselves back together again.

The beauty of the Sangha is it has the potential to support people who start going through this process of the dark night of the soul, during which people quite often feel like they're going in the wrong direction, doing the wrong thing and feel quite isolated because they see other people are relatively happy and they are not. They are feeling very discontent because the feelings that are coming up inside them are very discontented feelings, quite often hopelessness and helplessness, this feeling of isolation.

I went through the dark night of the soul alone, and it was really hard falling apart without support. Some of it was done in Perth, some of it was done in England, some of it was done in Italy, and some of it was done in Byron Bay. It was definitely an undoing process and in recognising that, because I actually had been trained, it wasn't stopped. I didn't try and put myself back together, I didn't try and survive it, which is what most people do. Unfortunately, in trying to survive it, they put themselves back together, they develop more coping mechanisms, they repress more of their wounding and they miss the boat.

The Sangha allows you to have friendships and friends who will support you through this process as you come apart, but it's not easy. It's really quite difficult. You see, your personality, your ego base, was built on foundations that are not very solid. Most people create a raft of who they think they are, and they live on this raft of who they think they are, which isn't real in any way, shape or form. They live in this and present this to the world and to some degree they believe themselves to be this. If they're honest with themselves, they know it's not true but most people aren't that honest.

This raft keeps them above their pain body, so it stops them feeling what is actually underneath, whatever wounding is underneath. The raft has a series of defence systems and coping mechanisms. So, when you meet adults, you're meeting a raft. You don't really get to know a person unless you've lived with them for about six months, and they've actually been under pressure, then you get to see what they're really like, otherwise, you meet the raft, you don't really meet the person.

Now in Mystery School, that raft is being challenged, it's being undone because it's actually in the way of knowing yourself as truth. So, Adyashanti talks about Satsang being a process of destruction. It is. It is the destruction of this false raft that you think you are and what you present to the world and when this starts breaking down, you have an identity crisis because the reference points that are held in this raft of who you think you are, get demolished. You're probably not this nice person that you thought you were. There are a lot of things inside this raft.

So, when meeting people, I'm meeting a raft, and I pretend that the raft is who they are because they're doing that. Well, a lot of people don't pretend, they think they are the raft. I know they're not the raft. It's not who they are. I actually have enough sensitivity to feel what's underneath the raft, so I know what they're hiding from. I know what their wounding is and it is across the board, it's not just you, everybody is like this.

When I was a publisher, before I began undoing the raft that made me up, I had a really strong raft. Very, very strong businessman personality, "Bigger than Ben Hur"-type raft that was practically impenetrable, and it was deadly because it was well-trained. That raft had to break down. It was in the way, big time. One of the reasons I gave away my businesses is because I could see the raft, I knew it wasn't real. I could see the defence systems. It was like wearing a suit of armour and I just could not get rid of it. Every time I took it off, it would be back in a flash and it was related to my business life because I was a warrior; a businessman warrior.

Anyone who got in my way, I just went straight through. So the process for me was undoing this raft and it was a very, very difficult process. I gave my companies away and became a vagabond.

I travelled around Australia as a vagabond for four years, deliberately, to undo everything, to find my heart, because the armour was actually keeping me away from my heart. But in the process, I went through devastating days, devastating nights and devastating weeks of discomfort because of what had been repressed in my life. Particularly as a child, when I was in boarding school. The feelings of abandonment and the injustice of the way it was all run there. It was difficult to deal with all this by myself and I realised that the Sangha has the potential to support people through this process because I don't think many people make it through. I think most people cop out and build another raft. Repress what they have coming up and put themselves back together in some way and try to make their life work, instead of allowing the raft to be destroyed.

While you have a raft, in other words, this thing you've created that's full of defence systems, you can't truly relax, you can't truly let go, because it takes energy to keep the raft going, because it's false, it's not real. It takes energy to keep maintaining it. It takes no energy at all to be a nobody, but the raft is a somebody and it takes energy to continue being that somebody that you present to the world and you present to yourself.

Now if you really want to relax, you can't be a somebody, you can only be a nobody. So, before enlightenment, I was a nobody and I could relax and be at ease pretty much all of the time because there was no raft to take care of. It had been destroyed through the process of undoing.

The process of seeing through beliefs, the willingness to meet whatever pain body came up with a warm welcoming. The Vishrant who was before, even before enlightenment, had been destroyed. The Vishrant who was a naturopath and a psychotherapist was nothing like the Vishrant who was a businessman. Very, very different people, because the raft that made Vishrant the businessman had been demolished, had been destroyed. Vishrant the naturopath and Vishrant the psychotherapist was a nobody, wasn't trying to prove anything to anybody, wasn't looking for approval from anybody, was actually at peace within himself. He wasn't trying to hide anymore, or avoid anything inside himself anymore, he was at peace. Of course, that kind of being in the world is the right way to support enlightenment – there was nothing in the way. My mind had mastered surrender, it had mastered let go, it had mastered acceptance. Whatever came along was okay, and this was done over a period of probably around 11 years.

So, you're going to fall apart. If you stay in the Sangha, that's going to happen. The false you is not going to survive the process, and it will be messy, and it will be unpleasant. This is the case for all seekers who truly get into higher consciousness. The raft keeps you in lower consciousness, the false one that you present the world with who you actually believe to be yourself, is in the way. It does keep you in lower consciousness.

It is very valuable to be a member of the Sangha because it will support you when you go down, and it will support you when you're up. That's why I'm constantly fostering your friendships with each other because I know how hard it's going to get for you and in the past, so many people have run away when things became hard because they didn't want to face what was coming up. They didn't like the feelings of hopelessness, separation. They didn't like the feelings of pain, which happens. As the pain body comes to the surface, you get to feel it, your identity gets demolished. Who you think you were, or are, gets demolished. This happens to all seekers who go higher in consciousness. That leaves you in a position of relaxation and rest, which is the right position for enlightenment because your mind has mastered surrender on the way through; it has mastered let go. So, the people here with you are your support crew for a very rough ride that all seekers go through. I'm constantly chipping away at your rafts because that's the obstacle in your way of knowing who you really are, of knowing yourself as truth.

Now if I'm taking away your rafts, which are your defence systems and your coping mechanisms that hold your pain body down, well your pain body is going to come up and the reference points as to who you think you are will get challenged. You're going to have an identity crisis until you're absolutely 100 per cent okay with being a nobody, going nowhere. Just here. Just here.

Any questions, any statements, any challenges to this teaching this evening?

~

S: You said you went through the dark night of the soul on your own. How did you know you were on the right track?
V: I didn't. I was lost a lot of the time.
S: So, what motivated you to keep going?
V: It's not in my nature to give up.
S: So, to your ego, it must have felt like just being ruined. How did you make it okay?
V: I became willing to die. Knowing that higher consciousness required death, death of the ego, which is unconditional surrender and I just allowed that to occur. I didn't try to survive.
S: It's a real non-doing then that you're talking about. Not trying any trick.
V: No. No coping mechanisms, no conniving.
S: I remember when I was very disturbed one time. I called you and you said, "There's just pain here, there's nothing to think about," and my mind was just pedal to the metal, just scrambling to make it better and you were like, "No, there's nothing to think about. There's nothing to figure out. There's just pain." I have no idea how you made it through.

~

S: How important is being grounded?
V: Extremely important. That's why I walked around Australia without shoes on, so I could be very grounded in my body, by feeling my feet. When we put our awareness on a part of our body we get grounded in our body. If we keep our awareness on that part of the body, we get grounded permanently. In wearing no shoes for four years walking around Australia, I became grounded in my legs and in my body because there was something in me that intuitively knew I needed to be very grounded.

I took advantage of railway tracks whenever I could, walking barefoot on railway tracks. Because when you're on a railway track, walking on the line, you have to be present. You have to be aware. You have to be aware of where you're treading and that was one of my practices; walking on railway tracks and being aware of my body.

S: Would you say that being grounded and aware helped you through the process?

V: It helped me keep away from the insanity of my mind. You see, when feelings come up, particularly if they're bad feelings, negative feelings and emotions, quite often the mind will start a story up about what it thinks has caused it. Now the story is not real, the feelings are because it's energy leaving, but the story's not real. Now if you're not grounded in your body, you're likely to start believing the story, and now you're lost again and you're creating more wounding again.

S: You said you spent time walking along railway tracks as a practice. In that time walking around Australia, was everything in your day devoted toward practice?

V: A lot of it was, yes. A lot of it was devoted to mindfulness. Mindfulness is simply being present to what's real. Whether it was my footfall or the feeling of the wind against my face or the sun on my skin or the cold of the winter because I wore very little clothing or my feet on the ground. It was about being present to what's real rather than being present to dream, which is what we think.

S: With all those practices, there would have been very little time left to think.

V: I wasn't interested in dreaming. My mind was already well trained. It was very good at analysing and getting things to happen, but I didn't want to live there anymore. It was very good at problem-solving. I simply didn't want to live in my head anymore; I didn't want to be a problem-solver for the rest of my life.

~

S: I really liked the discourse; it reminded me of my first couple of years here when you began dismantling my raft. Just how false the idea of my "self" was and how I resisted. I feel humbled. You talk about repressing and building another raft. On some level, I feel more defended.

V: Well, it's usually the resurrection of the old raft rather than the building of a new one.

S: You see me as resurrecting the old raft?

V: Yes. You aren't willing to feel pain, so you build the raft to protect yourself.

S: How do I not do that?

V: It's always up to you. I can show you the way. In other words, the door is open for you, but only you can step through and you're actually unwilling to step through, so I wait for you until you're willing.

~

S: What is it that you mean when you talk about realising that you know nothing? What is it that you don't know?

V: I love living as Beingness. As Beingness, there is no interest in living in a mind full of knowledge, there's no freedom in that; it's like living in a library. The preference is for wonderment, and when you don't know, you can be in wonderment like a little kid, but when you think you know, you're holding onto something and it's hard to be in wonderment. So I don't know.

S: I notice in me a failure pattern. There's an arrogance in me where I pretend I know when I actually don't. Is that just covering pain?

V: It could be covering wounding around low self-worth, valuing yourself through what you think you know when you don't. Arrogance is usually a defence system.

S: It's definitely a failure pattern. It keeps getting shown to me on many different levels.

V: It's always good to be a beginner. No one is going to give you a hard time for being a beginner, but you'll get a hard time if you pretend to know and you don't, and you get it wrong.

~

S: I too very much liked the discourse on the dark night of the soul; I've been feeling that way for the last couple of weeks. It makes sense to me when I'm listening to you talk about rafting and the rebuilding of the raft. I noticed today feeling kind of miserable and easily triggered. The identity I build for myself is usually a future goal for myself, which is one of the ways I prop myself up, but I'm not using it at the moment and my wounding and sensitivity feels like it's getting touched much more.

V: Yeah, I'd say that's absolutely true for you. That it is all coming apart and your pain body is coming to the surface. I think that's exactly what's happening, and it will pass, but you don't know when because you don't know how much is there. Sometimes it's like peeling an onion, you go through one layer and you go, "Yahoo!" And then something triggers you and you find another layer, but at the centre of the onion is nothing and eventually, if you keep peeling, you get to nothing.

S: Did you find many ways to just be?

V: No, I'm always being. I don't live in the personality, I live in Beingness. Another way of putting it is I live in nothingness, as nothingness, and it's very beautiful. When the ego thinks of that, it might have a negative idea of it, but it's not negative. It's very beautiful to just be, to be nothing. It's very beautiful.

S: As you spoke today, I felt guarded against feeling unlovable and how I do that is with my humour and trying to stay above everything by jumping onto future problems, moving quickly to stay away from all that fragility and feeling unlovable. It's like when I'm in the company of others, I don't want to be in my stuff because it's uncomfortable and I feel like I'll be bad company. So, it really feels like I'm going the wrong way.

V: Yes, it definitely feels like you're going the wrong way when you get into your stuff. I first started with personal growth, which is about becoming bigger, better and more powerful, and that feels like the right way all the way, but when you get into spiritual growth it's a little different because you're stripping down the bigger, better and more powerful. You're taking away the false. So, you get into the stuff that you haven't really dealt with, particularly from your childhood, and it's unpleasant. It can be unpleasant for quite a while, but if you're interested in higher consciousness, that's the game. It is about becoming less than, not more than.

S: You often speak about trying to lift everyone.

V: Because I can.

S: Was there a period when you had to put that aside?

V: To give you an idea, I was where you're at now when I was about 28. That's around 35 years ago. There's a big difference here now, isn't there?

S: So, back when you were going through your dark night of the soul.

V: It hadn't really begun yet, it was just beginning because that's when I stopped doing the bigger, better more powerful groups and started the "undoing the Vishrant" groups, you see?

S: So, is there like a shift in attention in that it's about watching for defences and keeping them down?

V: No, I recognised that I'd moved into a new game. I recognised that I had done very well in the bigger, better and more powerful game, and now there's a new game presenting itself which required a new set of rules and the rules weren't the same, so I had to learn the rules. It was about undoing, not about doing up and becoming bigger and better, but becoming less than, which meant undoing everything. It's like going naked, and unfortunately, when we start undoing our coping mechanisms, our belief systems and our defence systems, quite often underneath there's a pain body.

S: With our new centre, Restful Waters, opening up and the opportunity for new courses to be run...

V: Those courses will always be about undoing, really. If you really look at what yoga is, it's about undoing. I mean, people can get huge ego trips around it, which is the wrong direction completely, but yoga is about undoing, counselling is about undoing, meditation is about undoing, Satsang is about undoing. The centre is a place of undoing; everyone is carrying way too much.

S: So, I can feel that thing of rebuilding a raft. It's like everything I go into carries a sense of building up and re-shielding myself.

V: Well, that's your old patterning coming into play, that's your default armour.

S: So, what do I need to do to approach things differently?

V: Have a different goal. My goal was to be open because I saw that the people who had higher consciousness were wide open. They weren't defended, they were absolutely open; and so my goal was openness and I practised openness. Openness destroys the ego.

S: This morning I practised yoga and meditation and I felt so much happier for the first part of the day. Is this rafting or is this something else because as I'm practising, I'm being very mindful?
V: Yes, you're actually out of your head for a while. Your head is a place where you get hurt because of the stories and the feelings that are in there, and when you practise anything that involves mindfulness, like yoga, you get relief from that. It's different from rafting, you're practising being out of the mind, which is a spiritual practice, to be present to reality rather than being present to the mind. I used to start every day when I was a businessman with an hour of meditation from six to seven. Pretty cool way to start. Sometimes it was a bit difficult when I had a hangover. [LAUGHTER]

~

S: I feel like for me, I raft on my ability to do things.
V: Yeah you do, you're a do-aholic.
S: So, how do I break that? Obviously, there are things I still need to continue to do…
V: That's true, but how the do-aholic manages to avoid is by starting a project here which they don't finish. Then they start a project over here, which they don't finish, while still doing the first project. Then they start a project here which they don't finish, while still doing this project and this project. Then they start another project over here which they don't finish, while still doing this project and this project and this project. Then they start another project over here. Now they have five projects on the go all at once. They can work as much as they want and never need to take a break and because there are deadlines attached to each project, it's always urgent. Now doesn't that sound familiar?

~

S: I went to a counselling session today and looked at shame, just the symptoms of shame, going silent and staying in the background and feeling disconnected, and I do feel disconnected to people most of the time. Though it does feel better to feel connected, disconnection is what I usually do. So, how can I just leave shame behind?
V: You have assumed that shame is the problem. That is your assumption, your diagnosis. After watching you for years now

deliberately telling stories that are very shameful, I see you get a great deal of joy out of it, over and over again. So, your relationship with shame is interesting if that's what you experience. It's possible, just possible, that you may be using shame as a defence now; something else to blame for your unwillingness to communicate, your unwillingness to play the game, your unwillingness to share and be a giver. Maybe you should have a look at that.

S: Yes. Yes, I will, I do feel guilty and shameful.

V: Oh, sure you do from time to time, but I'm wondering about shame with you. You enjoy being seen as shameful, being seen as naughty. You have a wicked sense of humour that you only show certain people. I know about that too. [LAUGHTER] You enjoy it immensely. If you can get someone to squirm at one of your stories, you love it.

S: Yes, I do. [LAUGHTER]

V: You can't be left with any excuses whatsoever for not being a giver, for not being a caretaker because as a man, that's the role you need to take, to be a man. Hiding behind anything makes you unworthy.

Restful Yoga

V: Welcome to Satsang. On the banks of the sea, Peter decided to follow Jesus. As they were leaving the village, someone came to inform Peter that his father had died. He asked Jesus if he could go back and bury his father and Jesus replied, "Let the dead bury the dead!" This is a very misunderstood passage. The dead are those who aren't interested in Truth, as far as those who are awake are concerned because they're living as the dead; they're not living as reality. They are living as something not real; they are living as an ego. What is real is your true nature, which is Beingness.

The "I", which most humans live as, is false, it is not real. It is not even in time. By the time it recognises itself, time has passed, and it's in the past. It is not in real time and it's made up of reference points usually based on past memory projected into the future. Once again, not real. In fact, it's dead.

So, Jesus said, "Let the dead bury the dead." Those who are not interested in Truth are seen by those who are awake as the dead, or asleep. They may think they're awake because they are conscious of what's in front of them, but they are asleep to their true nature, they're asleep to who they truly are, and therefore dead. They are living as something they are not, living as a false "I" and so there is a certain stuck-ness in that because there is a limitation in that. It is a huge limitation, actually. In knowing yourself as Truth, as Beingness, you are free. You are free from the mind, free from the body, you're free from everything. Nothing can actually touch you anymore. That is very hard for the "I" to even conceive of, but anybody here who has experienced themselves as Truth knows that to be true. What we really are cannot be touched, not possible, it's impeccable. But humans, being the way they are, project what they think, what they know, what their experiences are, onto everybody else. They also do this onto enlightenment, and somehow, they think they know what enlightenment is. Unless you've experienced satori, which is only a glimpse, you haven't got a clue. You can't have a clue because enlightenment doesn't have reference points. There are no reference points in enlightenment, none. You really are living in the unknown, as the unknown. In my experience, without any fear at all, none, ever.

This is what this Mystery School is all about, you finding yourself as this: living as this light that you truly are, rather than this darkness that thinks it is you because if you take time out to analyse the ego, it's not light, not really. So, yesterday, I was talking to a fellow about tuning in. He was tuning into his mind to try and work out what I was saying, and he was missing the light. He was missing what is here because he still thinks it is about collecting knowledge. He hasn't worked out yet that that is not the case. You tune in to what is here, and there is the potential of knowing yourself as Truth. So, someone who is awake usually has a gathering of disciples, students, people who are interested in becoming awake or people who are already starting to wake up.

I actually don't have any interest whatsoever in educating people. You can go to university, to the library, to Google and get educated. Education or the collection of knowledge isn't going to help you; it doesn't raise your consciousness levels one bit. It doesn't ever heal a wound one bit. Surrender is the key, and surrender has to be practised because you're not good at it. If you do not have a practice of surrender, you'll never be good at it. Meditation is the practice of surrender; you surrender your thoughts for what is real. In Buddhism, that would be the breath. When things go wrong in your life, instead of resisting, you practice surrender. You practice openness when you notice you are closed. It is only in practice that you will raise your consciousness levels. In that openness, if you tune in to what is here, you may find yourself as This because you already are This. There is just a filter in the way, the mind, the "I", no other problem, only that. Educating the "I" isn't going to help you. Teaching the "I" to surrender through practice will help you so there's no need to take notes.

Just practise letting go, practise acceptance, practise openness, practise surrender, practise tuning in to the energy field that is here and dying in it, which is what happened for me when I was with my teachers. I walked around the edge of the abyss for too long and fell in and became the abyss because I already was the abyss.

Any statements, any questions, any challenges to this teaching today?

~

S: Do you think it is possible for someone who has not had a satori, a clear direct experience of reality beyond the mind, to value what is beyond the mind?
V: No. It's not possible.
S: So, the valuing comes after, like, "what was that?"
V: Yes, it comes afterwards. There can be a very strong curiosity, but the love affair develops because of the direct taste. I had a very strong curiosity, but it wasn't until satori that the love affair developed. In that love affair, you become willing to die for it because it is so beautiful.

~

S: When you speak of walking around the edge of the abyss, does that mean being with teachers, meditating, and practising surrender, etcetera?
V: In a way, but the main way was seeing the emptiness, seeing the spaciousness, feeling the silence and stillness, walking around the edge of it, witnessing it. At some point, "I" fell in and "It" was me, there wasn't a witnessing of it anymore, it was me.
S: Was that because of self-inquiry?
V: Self-inquiry definitely helped, so did meditation, I also did a lot of other things: Tai Chi, Qigong, yoga. Lots of things helped.

~

S: I notice there is a profound energy at Restful Waters as well as around you.
V: Yes, anywhere Satsang is held an energy-field develops, a buddha field develops.

~

S: It seems Beingness is more accessible if I'm relaxed, if the mind's relaxed.
V: Well, what is relaxation? Isn't it a part of surrender, letting go so there's no movement?

S: You said that before awakening, you experienced a lot of space, a lot of silence?

V: I practised what I teach. There wasn't just suddenly an awakening; there was practice for a long time, from about 1982 till 1998, something like that. You know some people practise a little bit? I practised a lot because I loved it; loved meditation, loved yoga, and I loved openness. Openness was practised every time I found resistance inside me and the practice of meditation was done for hours every day. I didn't just come along and get lucky. The greatest practice of surrender was when things were going wrong. Instead of resistance or coping, the practice was of unconditional surrender.

~

S: Was there a point in your practice when the mind became silent most of the time?

V: Yes. It happened in the early days. The reason for that was simple; I was very present. I love the present moment so when I started meditating, I was already quite present to reality. Meditation for me was easy, I was not a dreamer. Within a few weeks, I started finding no-mind because being present to reality prepares you for no-mind in a way. No- mind means no dream, and I was already not interested in dream. In my life, it was too dangerous to be living in dream. I lived in a dangerous world.

Self-Acceptance

> Every part, the good, the bad and the ugly,
> has to be warmly welcomed, warmly accepted.
>
> VISHRANT

V: Welcome to Satsang. So, a lot of people who get into personal growth and spirituality try to eliminate negative aspects of their psyche, the ones that are kind of primal, and that's not a possibility. You can take away some of your belief systems, but you can't take away the human nature, the primal programming. So, what can be done is you can accept it. If you don't accept it, if you're in denial of it, it creates a schism in you: the part that's denying and judging it, and the part that's being judged and denied.

You can't ever really rest inside yourself when you're not in acceptance of yourself, and the thing about these negative aspects of human nature is they do make up who you are as an "I". Without them, you wouldn't have the same personality, you wouldn't have the same drives and you wouldn't have the same position in life. It's just that some of them need to be a little disciplined, that's all, because they can cause trouble. That doesn't mean that they're bad or they're wrong, and if we judge them as bad and wrong, we create this schism in ourselves: the part that's being judged and the part that's doing the judging. Very difficult to really rest with that happening; very difficult to find any kind of rest because you're against yourself, you're not your own best friend. You're partial, and the chances are, if you're going to judge yourself heavily enough and not like these parts of yourself, you're going to create low self-worth. That then gives you a whole pile of wounding you'll spend your life avoiding.

Every part, the good, the bad and the ugly, has to be warmly welcomed, warmly accepted. When this occurs, it doesn't mean that you let the killer run the streets, or the thief steal or the liar lie. What it does mean is that you're whole now because you're holding yourself in acceptance. As a result of that acceptance, there is the potential for self-love. It's very difficult to have self-love when you don't like you, when you have negative judgments about you; very difficult. So when we're looking at foundations, this is where we have to look. How do we feel about us? How are we with us? Are we okay with us? Are we our own best friend? Or is there something else going on? It doesn't really matter how or why you learnt to judge yourself, it doesn't make a difference. It doesn't matter how or why you learnt to hold yourself in contempt. It doesn't matter. What matters is that you find a way to accept yourself exactly as you are so the war inside of you, the trouble inside of you, the schism inside of you, can rest. You can rest easily knowing that everybody is broken, it's not just you. Everybody has the same stuff inside them.

Human beings want to see themselves as so civilised, so without sin, so holy, but really this spacesuit is an animal; the mind is programmed for survival. It does all sorts of weird things and is capable of all sorts of horrific things. Of course, we don't have to give it permission to run, but it's in all humans. We love to demonise other people, but it's in us as well. If you haven't seen it in yourself, it's because you actually haven't looked. When you truly look inside you find the lot. Then, there is the possibility for you to find a way to accept that because it is okay. It might not be okay to run some of the things you find inside yourself in the world, but it's okay to have them. It's okay to hold them in tenderness, it's okay to accept them. To actually try to reject them, to deny them so you can be holy or a nice person, or at least see yourself in that light, is really ridiculous. It just creates so much suffering inside of you.

When we judge traits in ourselves as bad, when we hold them in contempt in ourselves, we're also likely to hold others who exhibit those traits in contempt as well. So, it doesn't allow us to love the world. How can we love the world when we're holding parts of it in contempt? How can we love the other? So, it all begins with self-love. Self-acceptance and self-love. How are you with you?

Sometimes, I talk about the ability to stand alone without leaning on people and standing alone in surrender, not in resistance. That's relatively easy if you're self-accepting and self- loving, it's reasonably difficult if you don't like yourself somewhere. You turn yourself into a beggar because you have low self-worth. It's difficult to stand alone in surrender, and in higher consciousness, you do need to stand alone in surrender.

The beginning of the journey is self-acceptance of every part of you, and that's up to you. No one can do this for you. Your parents can't do it for you, your friends can't do it for you and your partners can't do it for you. Nobody can do it for you but you. You're the only one who can find a way to be loving and tender with you, with every part of you, to find a way to love the one who fails, the one who lies, the one who steals, the one who wants to kill and the one who betrays. All of the aspects that maybe our society doesn't like and accept. What our society likes and accepts doesn't matter; it's about you, it's about your self-acceptance, it's about your self-love.

You want to go higher in consciousness? You find a way to love you and the thing about that is if you really find a way to love you, if you find a way to accept yourself and open yourself enough to love yourself, that love overflows. Instead of looking for love outside of you, you become the well, you become the well of love and then others can come and get loved by you. They can receive love from you because you're overflowing with love. You're not a barren desert trying to get love outside of yourself. You yourself are the well and it begins with a warm welcoming of whatever you find inside yourself. A tender okay-ness with whatever you find inside yourself.

Of course, that also involves having a look. If you don't bother having a look, well you're not going to see what it is you may or may not be against inside yourself. You have to have a look. You have to examine your psyche, you have to examine how it is and then accept it. Life becomes way, way more beautiful when you like you; when you are your own best friend.

Any questions, any statements, any challenges to this teaching this evening?

~

S: So, for me personally, I try to accept me as I am now, but I also recognise that there is room for improvement in different areas as well.
V: Oh dear. [LAUGHTER]
S: As you say, everyone is broken. I'm happy with how I am at this point in time.

V: Totally?

S: At this point in time, yes, but how I am is not necessarily how I want to be in the future.

V: Any statement followed by the word "but" usually negates the statement. You see, if we really want to rest, we have to be okay with ourselves as we are now, forever. The moment we start bringing in the future, we've left the now and gone into a dream that's not real and more than likely, you're still judging something here. I'm talking about a full stop of the judgment which doesn't mean that we can't actually improve ourselves, I'm not saying that. It's just that this idea that we're going to fix ourselves somehow later can keep us away from the total acceptance of what's here now, and this needs to be seen because this is the way the mind tricks itself. Are you truly okay with your brokenness, with whatever's not functioning 100 per cent, with what you'd like to improve, or not? Because this one here, this mind, both our minds, these are very slippery characters, and every human being has a very slippery character up here. It has to be seen, what it's truly up to.

What happens when it takes you away into a future dream? What happens? We have to see what that actually means. Does it mean we're in total acceptance and resting inside of ourselves now, or does it mean something else? For me, it means something else.

I'm perfectly broken, now, and it's okay. I've been perfectly broken my whole life, yet I've been involved in changing things, basically removing programs, but from a place of absolute acceptance, which means a place of restfulness and a place of openness, and this is tricky. You've got to really look at this closely and see if you are truly, truly open and in total acceptance of what is here, or is the mind fooling you?

S: But if you are truly in that state, completely, you will see no need to change, so you will not even initiate any improvement or anything that will remove patterns that creates problems because if you are so perfectly in acceptance, there is no need to remove them.

V: That's what the mind tells you and that's another one of its little tricks. It tells you that if I'm in total acceptance, I won't change. So, people refuse to go to total acceptance because they want to change, and what's more, quite often the people who do this also use negative motivators to get themselves to change and wound themselves further. I'm telling you this doesn't work. It just wounds you; and even if you do improve yourself and you do change, there's a part of you that's still not accepting, and its programming is not to accept. If you slow down enough through meditation and watch the mind, you'll see what I'm saying.

If you just go to the logical mind, you'll think, "Ah ha, this works, that doesn't work." But when you really slow down and watch the mind from a detached space, you'll see how tricky it's being and that there's never going to be contentment for as long as you think that somehow you have to improve yourself later. That does not mean you can't improve yourself, I'm not saying that, but unless you're a meditator, you may not realise what I'm saying – that the mind's non-acceptance of itself is the problem, and that realisation is the beginning of higher consciousness. So, you go to any monastery or ashram in the world and they'll teach you to meditate, so you can actually get this detached witness, so you can truly see what your mind is doing, not what it thinks it's doing but what it's really doing. Do you get what I'm saying? I ask because I used to think like you.

S: I do to some extent, but if we look at your example, when you have in the past, been in a state of complete acceptance, what has allowed you then to motivate you to change?

V: I developed a witness that watched my mind. The first thing I removed was worry. I noticed that my mind worried, so the silent witness was like the catcher if you like. So, that was the first pattern that was put in, this pattern of watching the mind. The second pattern was the pattern of stopping the mind, not thinking about it, not analysing it, just stopping it. Just stopping the worry, so worry will arise, the watcher will see it. The silent watcher will see it and this other pattern will come in and stop it. This is discipline, and unless we develop discipline through our childhood, through our teenage years, the mind won't do this.

The only way you can change the patterns in your mind is through discipline. If you don't have a pattern of using discipline, you won't use it. If you go into an ashram or a monastery, they teach you how to discipline your mind, how to watch the breath in Buddhism, and not move away from it, stay with it. When the mind comes in, you come back to the breath. You learn the discipline of staying with the breath and then stopping the mind if it comes in, and you're developing a mind pattern that becomes a default pattern. After a certain amount of time, the pattern becomes default.

I've had a witness of my mind since I was a teenager. In other words, I've had detachment from my mind since I was a teenager. I've had the program of stopping since I was a teenager. Now that pattern can be applied to any program in the mind; not just worry, any program, but if you don't have that pattern, if you haven't developed the ability to discipline the mind, well, you've got a bit of a problem. You're going to have to practise until you get it. It usually takes about two years to develop a default pattern, in my reckoning, in my understanding. That's up to you.

That particular pattern was then applied to victim-orientated thinking. Every victim- orientated thought that arose was spotted by the silent witness. I came from a victim- orientated environment, so I was programmed to be victim-orientated; the next thing was to stop it. No analysing, no diagnosing, stop it. Do not entertain victim-orientated thinking. It is a negative thing to do; it turns you into a weak character because you're being a victim of life and you're stabbing yourself. So, that was the second pattern that I applied this discipline to. By this stage, it was automatic. If I applied it to anything in my mind, it started to happen because it was default patterning. Do you understand? It wasn't done through discipline; it was done through default patterning. So, many years later, I decided I had a bit of a criminal mind, I had dishonest thoughts. The witness watched it; the mind caught it and stopped it. Every dishonest thought that arose in the mind was seen and stopped, until they didn't come any more.

S: So, your witness was not at ease with seeing those things?
V: Absolutely at ease. It's just a witness, just like a camera, like a video camera. It doesn't judge, it's non-judgmental in that it doesn't judge it as bad. It just witnesses what is and then another program is triggered to stop it.

S: So, it's the other program that is not content with how you are?
V: No, you're projecting an awful lot onto programming. We have dozens, hundreds of roles inside of us. This is a non-personal role and so is the stopper. It doesn't get involved in analysing, doesn't get involved in anything, just does its job. Like a set of traffic lights: they have radar on them, some kind of sensor that detects cars, that's the watcher. It's not personal, it detects the car, then the light changes. That's the stop, red light comes on. It's not personal, there's no judgment here, it's already over. The judgment was done ages ago, "I'm going to stop this because I don't like it." That's when the judgment was, but that was only for a very short time.

Maybe with worry, it was instant, as it was seen. There's a book called The Handbook to Higher Consciousness, and in it, this guy talked about worry and all sorts of different things, and it just really dawned on me: I do not want to suffer for the rest of my life entertaining something that I don't have to. Since 19, I haven't done any worrying. Well, that's 48 years, what's that worth? That's 48 years of not worrying. Not worrying! I don't worry. It is because of the silent witness which is non-personal, and this is developed in meditation. This is what they teach in ashrams and monasteries. Then I have a stopper, not a negotiator, a stopper. It just stops it, like a red light. Stop. I was of the strong opinion that I could be very successful in the material world if I worked on my failure patterns, and so at 19, I started looking for failure patterns in myself, in my psyche. The first one was worry. What a great failure pattern that is, it takes you nowhere. The second one was victim-orientated thinking, so those were the first two to be removed.

Now there's a whole pile of other patterns as well like excuses for failure. That was seen, witnessed, stopped. Any excuse for failure was removed because any excuse for failure pretty much guarantees you're going to do it again, it's just how the mind works. So, that was stopped. You won't find me having any excuses for failure, because the program has actually been removed. This is how you remove programs. It is not personal, it is non-personal. It's from a mechanical part of the mind that becomes default. Does that make sense?

S: Going back to what you said, the judgment was made earlier…
V: But the judgment was, "This is not a good thing for my life, so I'll stop it." You see, you're looking at things from a negative place. It's like when I see someone with something that's not working: it's not seen from a place of closure or negativity, there's just looking, and this is just what is, this is just behaviour, this is just what humans do, and I know that it can be changed or not changed, and I don't mind if it is or it isn't changed. I had the same attitude towards myself; it's an openness rather than a contraction. The problem we have with looking at ourselves is that we tend to look from contraction, and that doesn't work because it hurts us. We can learn to look at ourselves from openness, and in openness comes love. Man, then it's a whole other world when we start changing things. It is from a place of acceptance, it is from a place of love, it is from a place of beauty, not from a place of heavy judgment. Don't judge yourself. You know? Love yourself. I'm trying to teach this way of being in the world which is loving to yourself, which then goes out from you and loves the world. If you can't love you, how can you love the world?
S: I don't disagree with that one bit. What I was saying is that I view that I accept myself…
V: I don't agree with that. Can I tell you why? You are not at peace inside yourself.
S: Not 100 per cent, but I don't think anyone who's not completely enlightened could be.
V: No, no, this isn't true. I've been in acceptance of myself totally for at least the last 30 years, maybe more. Awakening only happened 21 years ago, so that's not true. It's just that all of us, because of our religions, our societies, what we grew up with, have a lot of trouble accepting ourselves because of all the judgments that are being put on us. I was very fortunate to have seen this and to have started removing them whilst very young. A certain peace was found inside myself as a result. It's very hard for people to find peace in themselves if they don't like themselves, if they don't accept themselves.

So, you don't have to be fully enlightened to be in full acceptance of yourself, that's just not true. I just removed all that patterning. I didn't buy it; I started not buying it at school. All the heavy judgments, the Christian judgments of right and wrong, good and bad were seen as poison, as this is how you cripple people so you can control them through guilt and fear. I didn't like that, because I'm into freedom. If you can't love yourself, if you can't accept yourself as you are, it's hard to be into freedom because somehow, you're holding a part of yourself in contempt. There's a part of you that's a prisoner of you, that's not being liked, that's not being held in tenderness. You're looking at it from a rational mind, I'm looking at it from meditation and if you go slow enough inside of yourself, you'll find what I'm saying is true.

I don't want you to believe me. If you go into meditation, into that silence, and look, you'll see what I'm saying is true. Then you will see for yourself, then it will become your knowing, not something I'm trying to teach you. That's what I'm doing here. I'm actually trying to get people to have a look inside themselves so they can find this for themselves. I don't want anyone to believe me, but I know the traps because I've already been in there. I know how tricky the mind is, the different excuses it can come up with for not accepting itself, because I've seen them in myself, and I'm trying to pass that on.

How are we going?

S: Yes, I'll have to sit with it for a while.

V: Ah good. Sit is good. Meditate. Stay with it. Watch the mind. Develop a silent witness and stop any negativity. The way of the heart is so beautiful, but it's so difficult for people because they don't like themselves and it's so important to find a way to like yourself, as broken as you may be. Now, not later, now! Because you might not be alive later. If your program is to put things off till later, if that's your program now, that's what you'll do later as well. We do run true to our patterning. Everyone does. Everyone is on railway tracks.

I've been in the business of trying to change people's programming for 30 years now. It's difficult. It is difficult to create new default patterns in people. Everyone thinks they can change really quickly, and with a certain amount of willpower, they can temporarily. But for something to become a default pattern, where they don't have to put any discipline into it, to truly change, that takes a long time. That's what I got into when I was a teenager, but I used discipline. I gave myself absolutely no choice. Nothing was going to get past that silent witness; nothing was going to get past. It was going to be stopped. The hardest program I changed in my mind was dishonesty, because I came from a background that was dishonest. We lived by the 11th commandment: Thou shall not get caught! To stop the dishonest thoughts was the hardest thing I did, but it stopped after a few years of, "No, no, no," and it's not done from harshness or negativity. It's just a program that doesn't entertain it, from a place of lightness inside myself, not darkness.

S: That judgment about yourself that's negative, is that a default pattern?

V: All patterns are default if they're running automatically without you thinking about them. Most humans operate about 80 to 90 per cent of the time from default patterns, they're not actually really thinking about what they're doing. Like riding a pushbike, you don't think about it, you just ride. I notice when ironing clothes, there is no thought about it, just ironing. Signing my signature is automatic; no thought about it. How much do we really have to think about, really? See, my mind has been silent now for 18 years. I don't do much thinking at all, maybe during a day, one per cent of the time? Probably not that much.

But we think we have to be thinking all the time. As adults, we've already been programmed to do just about everything without thinking. We don't need to live in our heads anymore. We did when we were kids to some degree, to learn all the things we had to learn, but as adults, we don't, and as a meditator, I learnt not to. I learnt to be here with you, with my hand, with reality, not in dream. I love reality. I see dream as imprisonment.

~

S: In myself, I notice that I don't particularly like being ungrounded. It's not that I hate it, I know it's just a part of my psyche at the moment and I'm trying to put in more practices to become more grounded, but I find that in others when I...

V: You're not with me when you're talking. You're looking at the roof, you're over there. I'm here and I'm with you 100 per cent. You're not even 40 per cent with me, that doesn't work. Spirituality is the world of reality, not the world of dream. A lot of people think spirituality is somewhere else; a true spiritual teacher is present, every moment, present. It's not about la-la land; that's where everyone else is living. It's about being ruthlessly present to reality and ultimately ruthlessly present to Beingness. You weren't present with me when you were talking. When people are like that with me, I don't feel like talking with them. You want to talk to me, you talk to me. I'm here, I'm alive.

~

S: I really like how you make it so simple and so crisp and clear when spotting something that doesn't work and stopping it.

V: Well, do you want to win or lose? That was the thing about being a teenager, wanting to win. I dropped out of high school in fourth year. I wanted to be an entrepreneur, but I knew to be an entrepreneur, my failure patterns had to be removed, so they were. Within nine years of leaving school, I had retired. No need to work anymore if I didn't want to, not really, because if you haven't got failure patterns, it's pretty hard to fail, you know, especially if you have reasonably good mentors, which I had. I found businessmen who were switched on and learnt from them. If you haven't got failure patterns, it's pretty hard to fail. By 26 years of age, I was turning over millions.

S: It's like you just streamlined yourself. Streamlined, and streamlined, and streamlined. No dramas, no need to really analyse, if something doesn't work, it doesn't work, it's gone.

V: Yeah, I don't like living in the head. I like reality, knowing what's behind me all the time, being that alive, you know? That's mindfulness.

~

S: I'm currently sitting through a counselling course and what you're talking about largely lines up with what they call The Paradoxical Theory of Change, where basically they state that in order to change something, you first have to accept it, otherwise, the

mind is tricky, and it will hide and lie to you and any attempts to change will most likely be unsuccessful.
V: Well, this is something I found in meditation. It isn't something to learn from a book because if you borrow the knowledge, it's not yours, it's borrowed. You need to find it for yourself, inside of you.
S: You were talking about ending worry. At that time, you didn't have a strong meditation practice. It was just willpower alone and your drive to succeed?
V: I was involved in Alpha-Level Thinking. I don't know if you know what Alpha-Level Thinking is? You create a workshop inside your mind and you create the discipline in that workshop. I developed a workshop and had a strong discipline inside my mind that witnessed and stopped worry until the new pattern became solid.
S: So, for us you just prescribe meditation?
V: Well, the practice of meditation teaches you discipline, you know? If you have a practice of meditating every day, it's teaching you discipline.
S: The program to repress…
V: To repress what?
S: Say you're brought up with particular beliefs that programmed you to repress sexuality, as it's taught that it's not okay. With repression you have the pattern, you see something, and you stop it. The pattern of the witness is already there…
V: Well, if you want to see what's inside of yourself, you have to become still, you have to become quiet, and you have to stop moving. Otherwise, you can't see. Meditation is about not moving; it's about becoming silent. If you come and hang out with me, you'll feel the stillness, but that's because of years of meditation. It was like that 35 years ago. The stillness was there because I'd already been meditating and I loved meditation; for an hour or more every day going into that silent, still, quiet, beautiful place, as opposed to analysing things. My mind is pretty good at analysing; I'm just not interested in analysing. I love that silent stillness and the knowing that comes through there.
S: Guilt, from my experience, is one of the most disempowering emotions there is, and it is the opposite of acceptance.

V: Yes, and it's damaging because you're beating yourself up and wounding yourself, but there's regret, which is not guilt. Regret is when you feel sincerely sorry for what you've been involved in, and you can do that from a place of acceptance, and regret is the great heart opener. When we're sincerely sorry for what we've been involved in, from a place of openness, it opens the heart right up. There's no beating up in it. So, I talk about dropping guilt and allowing ourselves to feel regret if it's there. Yeah, guilt is terrible, and the church sells it, but I stopped buying it because when I was a kid at school, they would try and guilt- trip me all the time. I wouldn't buy it. I was bad!

Meditation is the key to really see what's happening inside you.

~

S: If you find yourself desiring something quite strongly, is it an indication that you're not accepting yourself or your situation?

V: No, not really. It just means you're desiring something aggressively. I loved the space I found inside myself with meditation and tried taking that space into work and into relationships and even into partying, and that space is a very cool, beautiful space. People would try and disrupt it, but that's the world, you know? The world does what it does.

S: For me, I go through these phases where I get into self-growth, especially around business.

V: You can do that from openness, you don't need to do that from a closed space. Business is just common sense anyway; you just make more money than you spend.

S: I guess when you're making like $20 more than you spend...

V: Well, you just got to make more! For me the trick was simple with money: you just hang out with people who were really successful and let them tell you how to do it. Let them tell you the recipe for success, which is pretty difficult. Part of the recipe is clarity, clarity to see what's happening, and if you're living in your head, you don't have clarity. You've blown it because you're procrastinating and worrying – that just creates a mess in your head. That creates a density where you think you might be able to see thing,s but you can't really. You don't have clarity. You've got to have the clarity of a hunter; very crisp and fresh.

Also, you have to be total in whatever you do. If you decide to not be total you will fail because when it gets tough, you won't have the totality to follow through. I've watched so many people get business advice from different mentors and just not follow it. They think that somehow they know better, and arrogance is just a killer, it's just a killer. You go to a teacher and the teacher tells you to do it this way, you don't do it your way, you do it the way the teacher taught you. Then you'll succeed because the teacher wouldn't be teaching it to you unless it was a successful methodology. Your way, your arrogance, will be in the way of success.

You have mentors who are telling you which way to go. I wonder how much of their advice you're following, or do you know better? So many people think they do.

~

S: With regards to your earlier talk, I know for myself, programs and patterning can cause me to feel guilt around money...

V: How do you think I stopped guilt? I used the same discipline. There's a witness, guilt would start to arise and it was stopped. It's just a pattern, you see. What I didn't stop was regret, but guilt was stopped because after being brought up on it, I just saw it as tragic. It was a tragic way that the church that I was involved in tried to control people. Even my parents were doing it. They'd try to guilt-trip me as well. I'm not going to be controlled by guilt, it's over. You create a pattern that watches and stops it and it will stop it. After a while, it will stop coming because you're not entertaining it anymore, but if you don't keep up the discipline, you will fail. If you give it credence once, you will fail. You have to catch it every time, every time.

This is the discipline that you develop to be a successful businessman, or athlete, or musician, or artist, or anything in the world where you've got people doing well. They have discipline. If they didn't have discipline they wouldn't be doing well. Natural talent is not enough and in the world of higher consciousness, it's the same deal. It's discipline.

~

S: I have a question on self-acceptance. Quite often, if someone's not accepting me, then I am also not accepting myself, so I feel like no one is on my side...

V: Oh no! And you're so unacceptable a lot of the time! [LAUGHTER] I say that with all humour mate, you're okay, just a bit broken. Perfectly okay. If I was in a position where I needed your acceptance, I could never tell you the truth, it would stop me from being a good counsellor. If I'm worried about whether you'd accept me or not, how can I really be a good counsellor to you? I'd probably be more interested in protecting my own interests. I can't afford to be interested in your acceptance if I'm going to be of help to you because I'm going to tell you the truth.
S: So, if someone criticises me or something, then as a default I take their side.
V: Oh no! You take someone else's side against yourself? Wow! That's awful, I would stop that. Otherwise, you'll just get pushed here, there and everywhere by anyone who just doesn't accept you or accept your behaviour. Gosh, talk about easy to control!
S: I liked what you said about accepting programming that's just not working in order to succeed. I notice my non-acceptance around my lack of intelligence, I just want it fixed before accepting it, relentlessly want it to be fixed, and I can see the damage that it does inside of myself. I just know I've done it the wrong way for a very long time. Something I noticed recently, after receiving some feedback, is that there's areas where I am actually incompetent, but from the outside that's okay, it's not the worst thing in the world. But I project that people are judging me a lot and that's what keeps me from accepting myself. Does that make sense?
V: Yes, it makes sense; it means you're very easy to control. All they have to do is not accept you and you'll fall into line. There's no freedom in that, not really, is there? Find a way to love yourself as you are, to accept yourself as you are. Acceptance from others, if you chase that, you're just going to twist yourself into knots, into something you're not, to get their approval. It's horrible. What other people think of you is their business, not yours anyway, and they have the right to think what they want.

~

S: I like the talk around guilt. I see in myself I tend to get very nervous when there is a lot of attention on me.

V: So, you don't accept the nervousness when people put their attention on you? Why not? Maybe you need to examine that a little more closely, sounds a bit like a surface look. What is it exactly that you feel when people put attention on you? What brings this nervousness up? What are you actually frightened of or ashamed of? It would be good to actually have a close look and see the mechanics of this rather than just keep it at surface level.

S: Because I get things wrong.

V: What's wrong with being wrong? It's actually okay to get it wrong, it is, it's fine. It's not like you attempt to get it wrong, but it's okay to get it wrong because you're a human being and you're faulty like every other human being. It's okay to get it wrong. You make it okay to get it wrong and then you can rest with that, otherwise, you're going to have a problem because from time to time, human beings get things wrong. Every now and again even I get things wrong! I know that's really hard to believe, but I do. [LAUGHTER]

S: I guess there must be some kind of episode in childhood that has created this.

V: Going back there may help you, or it may not help you. There are different ways you can deal with it. If I was you, I would be looking at getting myself in a position where people are looking at me, where I'm being put on the spot, and examining my own internal process. Being more interested in what is happening inside of me than what they are doing, so I can actually see what's going down and then dismantle it. Once I've seen the mechanism of it, dismantle it. This was done when I started doing public speaking as a teenager because it's frightening talking to a crowd of people about things that you're supposed to know about, but may not. So at some point, you actually have to have a look at what it is inside of you that gets frightened, what it is inside of you that tightens up, and dismantle that. Otherwise, it's too difficult to do public speaking. It's too difficult to keep doing it.

S: At the party, you told me that I was very well dressed, and I felt put on the spot. I didn't like that.

V: You need to have a look at why. You need to go inside yourself and really examine how your mind is ticking, find out why it's doing what it's doing. Don't be ignorant of your mind. Find a way to know how it works. Ignorance is not bliss.

~

S: I found your conversation today very interesting.

V: Why? "Interesting" to me could mean anything.

S: There was a point you were describing how you need to accept something before you change something; the paradoxical theory of change. I found that really interesting and reflecting back on myself, especially around maturity, I spend so much time trying to hide and trying not to be seen as immature that I don't get to actually practice being mature. I miss the boat, it's really stupid.

V: Yes, but you're having a look and that's a great beginning. A lot of people don't look; they just run true to their default patterning whether it's mature or immature, they just run true to it. You're having a look, and this is the beginning of higher consciousness, to actually have a look. Then of course if you see something that's in the way of higher consciousness, you stop it. If you're not willing to execute that goal, not much is going to change because insight doesn't change your consciousness levels. Insight is just the invitation to do the work.

S: Yes. I also liked your point of having the witness and the stopper, and having those two roles working side by side, with no story.

V: No story whatsoever, no judgment, no negotiation. You treat what you're trying to get rid of like a terrorist in a way. No negotiation, but from a place of openness, from friendliness, not harshness, not hostility. We're just going to deal with it, okay?

S: I see I fail in that aspect because I do negotiate a lot.

V: Then you're lost in dream. Well, that doesn't work.

S: I'm just looking at how the self-acceptance ties in with co-dependent behaviour. I start seeking approval outside of myself from a place of non-acceptance.

V: It probably stops you from being a truly effective human being, because you can't stand your ground. Someone who's really, really free can stand their ground, in surrender, against the world, but if you're folding because you want people's acceptance, you can never do that, and the people you want acceptance from are probably not even thinking about you. They're more interested in their own journey, which is called self-obsession. At school, no matter what I did, I couldn't get acceptance from the teachers, so I just gave up. Not by going into apathy, just by stopping looking for acceptance, which was so cool because what an awful way to live, constantly selling out to get along; selling out on yourself to get along, to be accepted.

S: I heard you say that there's also a primal element there.

V: Well, there is a primal element to it. If we're not accepted by the tribe we die because we get ostracized, left out, and the wild animals or other tribes will get us, but as you get more conscious you can let that go. Let everything go. It's okay for the world not to accept you, particularly if you like you, and you love you; it really doesn't matter.

S: So, in self-acceptance, it drops away by itself?

V: Pretty much. Mind you, I wasn't interested in getting acceptance from people anyway. I could see really clearly that that was how you can be manipulated and controlled. You either like me or you don't like me, it doesn't matter, it's okay. I'm going to be me.

~

S: I found the part about being present to who you're talking to really applies to me.

V: Yes, I love the present moment; being present to whatever's happening, it's really cool.

S: I find interesting the relation here between being present and the forgetfulness that people have here about what they're talking about or what question they're about to ask. Is that a sign that people are not being present?

V: Well, I'm here, present right now with you.

S: But if you forgot what you were talking about with me, does that mean you would not be being present?

V: No, it would mean I'd forgotten what I was talking to you about while still being present with you. Present is being with you, just having awareness with you instead of with thinking. Quite a lot of people here, when they're talking with me, are actually with their own mind, and in a spiritual sense, that's a bit of a no-no. You're supposed to be present. Meditation is supposed to be every moment if you're really going to the higher levels of consciousness. That means being present every moment to reality. Depends on what you're into. I'm into higher consciousness, and my teachers in the 80s told me to be in meditation every moment. That means present to reality, what's real, every moment. So that was a goal of mine, but I was already into it anyway. I loved being present and didn't like dreaming.

S: To me, if I was not present with a person, it would be easy for my mind to wonder and forget what I was talking about. So, I'm wondering what is causing people to forget what they are saying when trying to have a conversation around you.

V: No matter what my personality is like, awareness is aware of itself inside of this body, which is enlightenment, and that creates an energy field that can melt people's minds. It can actually take their minds away, and it does. As a seeker, when I first came into contact with this energy field, it wasn't perceived. The next year when I went back, it blew my head off. It was the same energy, it's just that my mind was so strong as a businessman, it was actually defended against it. The energy here will melt your mind, it will relax you, it will wipe you, but that's the same with anyone who's awake. As a matter of fact, it's one of the indications that someone is awake. If it doesn't start occurring, then you're not with someone who's awake. How does that sound?

S: Well, it's not something I can automatically believe, but it's something I can accept and understand just the same.

V: Well, it doesn't sound like you've been around spiritual communities before, or Eastern spiritual communities before.

S: Well, some.

V: Any awake teachers?

S: Not person to person.

V: Okay. Awake teachers are rather rare in the West. In India, there's quite a few, in Thailand, other countries where these practices for higher consciousness occur, but in Australia, there's no practice towards enlightenment, not really. There's just the practice of belief and prayer, which is different. It's about becoming lighter and lighter and lighter. Basically, to stay awake, I can't have a story of me, and because there's no story of me, there's no thought. Most of the time my mind is just empty. I'm here, 100 per cent here, just empty. There's an energy field that's emitted here because awareness is aware of itself here, which is the same as anybody who is awake, but it doesn't occur in people who aren't awake. Does that make sense?

S: I can understand what you're saying.

V: If you study Hinduism or Buddhism, that's actually taught. It's said that's how it is. I've got a good way of talking about it, you tell him what it's like, and then you tell him, and you, and you (indicating different students to talk in turn). Because these guys are being affected by it right now. So, you tell him what happens.

S2: I'm sitting here with Vish and I feel very present, but at the end of each sentence I pretty much forget the sentence before because I'm so here and feel like I'm expanded by the energy.

V: And you?

S3: I feel quite alive and calm at the same time, staying present, but I, can't, find…

V: You see, I just stopped his mind from working; an awake person can do that, and it's not a trick. If you study enlightenment, Eastern style, you will find that this is one of the siddhis that people who are awake have. Not by force, simply by putting awareness on the person. You might find it strange, but this is commonplace amongst people who are awake. Does that make sense? You see he's lost it completely! And for you?

S3: Very peaceful and mind expanded, and I've sat with maybe five awakened teachers who have the energy field. Very spacious and quiet, so yes, there's a very great potential for me to not remember what I was saying.

V: And you, you don't feel it that much, do you?

S4: No, but what I notice is the ease of finding less mental activity. The conditions have to be right with a lot of physical activity before meditation to find this stillness.

V: And you, tell him, but don't look at me, you'll lose it!

S5: My, mind, is … Jeez! It's like …mmm…

V: And you, do you want to tell him?
S6: Really calm; just mind is really expanded.
V: You see as a seeker, I didn't go to teachers who weren't awake, couldn't be bothered, and there weren't any in Australia as far as I knew, so I had to go to America and live over there with teachers who were awake, and then to India. You see, there was no interest in being with someone who wasn't awake, because if you're interested in higher consciousness, why would you want to be with someone who wasn't awake yet? So, I lived in America for two stints of four months each, India for five months, Italy for five months, London for a while, chasing people who were awake. Someone who is awake has already done the work, otherwise, they wouldn't be awake. They know all the traps and if you can actually get to play with them, they'll show you where you're caught and help you see the way out. Someone who is still ego-based, who is not awake, can't do that because they're still asleep, they're still trapped. They're still unconscious. More students here can explain and we'll get the same results. The energy here is kept at whatever level serves best. If I turn it up too high, people can't talk very much, so I don't.

You experience yourself as somebody. I don't experience anybody here, no sense of self whatsoever, and this is part of awakening. The sense of "I" disappears completely because awareness is on itself or awareness is on Beingness, which is self, or awareness is on Truth, which is self. It's just different ways of saying the same thing. This happened here 18 years ago and has been like this ever since. People lose their minds and they forget what they're saying. It affects my mind as well, it affects this mind, it just blows it. I'm doing my best. Okay?
S: Thank you.

How to Deal with Shame

V: Welcome to Satsang. On the drive here, reflecting on what it is I like about my life, a comparison was necessary. The comparison was to my life before teaching. As a businessman for much of my early life, I was living quite differently, and the differences are really simple. My life now is spent taking care of other people instead of thinking about myself and taking care of me. It's pretty much that simple because before getting into service, I used to think about me, take care of me, and use people to take care of me. I used to take care of them because they were taking care of me, but it wasn't the same. There was no real beauty in it, there was no joy in it, there was no silence in it, there was no stillness in it. In vanity, selfishness, and self-obsession, there's never any stillness or silence.

When you start being in service to others and the story of you disappears, there's a lot of silence, a lot of stillness because you're not self-obsessed. Looking at what I like about the way I live now, it is that when I take care of others, there's no story of me. The mind is silent and still pretty much most of the time. If I could give a gift to somebody, it would be to give them this knowledge, that a life in service, which is the way of the heart, is the best way to live, and that if you truly look at a life that is selfish and self-obsessed, you can see clearly how you create your own suffering, which is absolutely unnecessary.

I was very fortunate to see this when I was 33, or around then, and changed my life to be one that could assist others in what they were doing rather than just feathering my own nest, so to speak. It's a hard thing to get people to understand though because the ego goes, "Well, what's in it for me?" and really, there's nothing in it for the ego; it's just a beautiful way to live, it's an honourable way to live. You can look at yourself in the mirror and really like what you see because there's something missing; the selfish one is not there anymore, the self-obsessed one is not looking back anymore.

Sometimes this is called the beauty way or the way of the heart, and it's different for every individual; it's not the same. What you do to become a giver could be completely different to your partner or anyone in your family or anyone you know. What suits you in the path of the heart suits you, and if you're interested, you'll endeavour to find that which suits you. For me, it meant giving up a career because it simply didn't suit. The whole organisation was based on making heaps of money for me, quite often at the cost of everyone else. I had to give that away and walk away from it because it was really clear that it was the wrong direction to go.

When we are looking at what direction in life to go, it involves us taking inventory of ourselves. What are we doing? What do we really want in life? Are we pursuing that? Are we doing it in a way that will be successful? Or are we a bit lost? I felt very lost realising that all the money I'd made and all the success I'd had was a waste of time, and that the only true beauty was love, and in that, I was bankrupt.

Looking around to find something to do was a journey that took a few years. Knowing that I couldn't go back into the management of people, being too good at using them to make money, something had to be found that I could do by myself in service to others and also something that would support my family and myself. There's no point in starving to death while you're on the path of the heart, but at the end of the day of work, I felt good because I'd been in service and actually tried, maybe not succeeded, but tried to make a difference in other people's lives; and the willingness was there to try again the next day, and the next day, and the next day. It didn't matter if I failed – I was just willing to try, and of course, in the beginning, I wasn't that good at it, so I had to try a lot.

If I could give you a gift, it would be this understanding and this knowledge because it is life- changing. All the beauty and all the joy in this world comes from being a giver and all the misery in this world comes from being a taker, and it's up to you which path you pursue. No one will ever make you do anything you don't want to do; it's up to you completely. You are the author of your reality.

Are there any questions, any statements, any challenges to this teaching or does anyone have anything they would like to talk about this evening?

~

S: You say that you fell into the best profession to be able to give to others, but how do we know what or how to give?

V: Gee, there was no falling into anything, it had to be found. Travelling around Australia for nearly four years, trekking around Australia looking for what I wanted to do, I was really lost for a long time. As I was going around, wherever I stayed, I tried to lift whoever I met in some way, tried to find a way to make their lives a little better, still not really knowing what to do because my main skills in life were in business management. So eventually, after realising more skills were needed at what I wanted to do, I went back to school and trained as a naturopath and as a psychotherapist to be in service, so I had some skills to help people, but that was quite a process and there was no falling into anything. It was a plan, it was a goal. It was a plan, and the plan was executed. It wasn't a mistake.

You want to know what to do? You just look for what you can do. We spend so much time looking for how we can help ourselves. Even if we took 10 per cent of that time into looking for how we could help others, we would find heaps to do, heaps of ways. I decided to try to lift every person I met in some way, to help in some way. Other people might find something to do with animals or helping the planet in some way. There are so many ways. What interests you? You have to find what interests you. Really, it's an attitudinal change.

~

S: At that stage… did your mind put up any resistance when you were asked?

V: No. It was the end of my travels and after wandering Australia pretty much as a beggar for a few years, there wasn't much of a problem with being seen as less than. Everybody I knew had seen me as a bum for at least two years. The Rolls Royce was definitely knocked out of me.

S: In talking about lasting, deep attitudinal changes you've referenced humility. Is that the cause of most attitude changes and let go?

V: Humility is simply a lack of self, a lack of the "I" really. When you look at it closely, it's just an absence of the "I" and it's not like you have to really humble yourself. If there's an absence of the "I", there is humility. The story of you is what makes you up. The lack of story, the absence of the story of you, leaves nothing there to be in the way. If you have a life where you're putting others first, where you are putting yourself aside, humility is just natural. It's when you're putting yourself first that there's a problem. When life's all about you, your problems, your story, your wants, your rights. When that's not there, there's just nothing but humility. Humility is really simply an absence of you.
S: When you do think, what does it tend to be about? Is it just practical things?
V: Yeah.
S: So, there's no needless daydreaming?
V: No daydreaming at all.
S: You said you were reflecting today. Do you do that often?
V: Not really. It's just that on the way here, as per usual, I had absolutely nothing to talk to you about, so a subject came into my mind, "Why do I like my life?" and that gave me a subject to talk about. Because so many people don't like their lives, and so why do I like my life? I have liked my life for a long time, for the past 25 years, because for 25 years I've been in service, and if I could give that to you as a gift, I would. So, the subject was delivered. The message was delivered.
S: With that question, "Why do I like my life?" I could say, "I like parts of my life, but I don't like all of it." Is the reason why I don't like all of it because I'm not in service all the time?
V: More than likely you're not in acceptance of what is. More than likely you're in resistance, in some way to what is, and as a result, you don't like it. When you start to practise acceptance of what is, it's easy to like things. The good, the bad, and the ugly can be liked, right?
~
S: Last year, at one of your meetings, you talked about surrender and practising it, and I have practised surrender since. What direction could I take now?

V: After turning 33, the realization that 33 years had been wasted in service of myself and not knowing how long I had left, the decision was made to find a way to be in service to others. Since then, I believe I have lived because of service to others. Before that, I considered my life had been wasted. So whatever time you have left in this life, the most beautiful thing you can do for you is to be in service, in some way, to others.

Part of being in service to others is not to live in your head because if you're living in your head, you're just self-obsessed. So, you get out of your head and you be there for others and the story of "you" will disappear and you'll find silence and stillness. You'll find the beauty of being because there won't be anything of you left anymore. How's that for opportunity?

S: It's just a way to get there. It's very complicated.

V: No, it's not complicated, it just takes time. It's really just an attitude. That's all it is; it's an attitude. There is another side to the attitude of wanting to take care of people which hasn't really been outlined. I didn't consider it worth living anymore to be a selfish man. What was the point of living anymore as a selfish man? I gave myself no choice and went into service. There we go. Every person on this planet is your brother or your sister and you can lift them in some way when you meet them if you wish to. It's up to you.

~

S: At work today, I arrived at a job and I was told what the problem was, and I created a plan for how to diagnose it so I could repair it, and I noticed that I went into hope about the outcome of my diagnosis. Is that hope a problem?

V: Anything that takes you out of the moment and takes you into dream is taking you away from truth. Dream or your mind is not real; it's not truth. The Buddha said that the two main obstacles in the way of higher consciousness for all human beings are hope and fear because hope takes you into a dream that is not real at all and fear takes you into a dream that is not real at all. Neither fear nor hope are real, yet people love to live in them. Abandon all hope, do not support fear, and stay present to the moment.

~

S: The sort of lifestyle changes you're talking about, moving into service, seem to require quite a conviction for the attitude change to take hold. What was it that had you realise that it wasn't worth living selfishly with the way you'd been living anymore? Was there an event or series of observations?

V: I remember being really cold and sitting in the water. I'd been sitting in the water for about 18 hours and there were two sharks circling me, and I realised that there wasn't much of what I'd done in my life that was worth anything. My life had been successful, but selfish with very little positive impact on any people, if any… more of a negative impact. In fact, I felt absolutely bankrupt even though I was quite wealthy, and I did not want to live like that anymore. The chance to live again after being rescued from being eaten by sharks was an event that changed my life incredibly because I took personal inventory. I had to look; what is my life like? What am I doing? Where am I going? What have I done? Was there any honour in what I'd been doing? What kind of a man was I? And I didn't like what was seen.

S: When you went from being a businessman to a bum…

V: It's easy, you know? It's harder to go the other way.

S: How did you feel, and in that action, what changes did you go through?

V: You know, it was a process that took a little bit of time and during that time period, there were lots of different emotional shifts about the situation because really I had to let go of my identity as a wealthy, successful young man. That was difficult because it also meant letting go of my friends and the respect I had from my peers. I went through a grief process of loss as I allowed those things to be taken away from me. There was a point where I felt really free of the responsibilities to take care of so many things because when you have nothing, you don't have to take care of anything. When you have things, when you own things, you owe responsibility to care of them, and so I felt very free, eventually. Just to be on the road with a backpack and a thumb was pretty cool; on the road to nowhere.

S: What would you say is the first step, the actual first step into higher consciousness from even like just success in the world, survival stuff? You were a businessman and you did very well, and you moved into something more than that, something beyond survival. What would you say is the very first step of that?

V: Taking up a meditative practice, the first step. If I had not been a meditator, I wouldn't have seen what I saw with the sharks. My mind wouldn't have been able to rest and just watch itself. Meditation allows that detachment, that clarity and that insight.

S: Couldn't you say that running a successful business is easier to attain than higher consciousness? Why is it so much more difficult?

V: I don't know if it's more difficult. It's similar, in that what works is totality. People who are willing to put their totality into whatever they're doing quite often succeed, and so, it is hard to be successful in business, but it's easy if you put your totality in. It's hard to succeed in higher consciousness, but it's easy if you put your totality in. It is partiality that causes failure in every field of endeavour.

~

S: Vishrant, did the people who you helped want to be helped?

V: Yep. Most of them paid for it.

S: Would you help people who didn't want to be helped? Just like being in service to others.

V: Not really. I recognized that to help people, there needs to be a welcoming. If there isn't a welcoming, it's probably the wrong place to be. You can set up an environment where you can be welcomed, but if the welcoming is not there, it doesn't really work in my experience.

S: So other than need, what would you say would be the best way to receive?

V: Well to be able to receive, you have to like yourself. The people who don't like themselves or who have low self-worth often have quite a problem with receiving because they don't feel worthy. As far as receiving is concerned, it comes back to liking yourself, being in acceptance of yourself. When you like yourself and you are accepting yourself and you respect yourself, there isn't any problem whatsoever with receiving.

~

S: I had a phone call today from an old friend of mine, someone I used to be friends with about 10 years ago, and it's the first person in a year who I've told what I'm doing for a living because I've been ashamed. She didn't care and it didn't faze her, but I've built up this story in my mind that I would be rejected or something because of it. You talked about how when you were a bum, after a couple of years, you almost got used to it, so it didn't faze you. I can't remember what you said exactly. How can I carry that with me because it was really nice to just talk about what I do and not come from a defensive place?

V: Well, it wasn't that I got used to it; the interest was in what was happening inside of me, if shame was felt or the feeling that something was not right. The interest was more in my own internal process. What was I resisting inside of myself? What defences were in play? What belief systems were in play? The mechanics of my own mind were much more interesting than I was ashamed or not ashamed of what I was doing. I wasn't really caring so much about what people thought as much as what was happening in my own psyche because I realised that what was happening in my own psyche, the nuts and bolts of my mind, was actually the problem, not what was happening outside of me. I was investigating the problem and any time we're not prepared to be seen in a certain light because we get frightened or it touches something, that's a place inside ourselves we have not been prepared to show up in, so it gives an opportunity to show up there and be with it and be okay with it.

S: I haven't seen to those depths. My vision is very out on what's happening outside of me and when I feel like something is being triggered, I know that's an opportunity to investigate, but I'm not wanting to use my mind, so I get confused about how to investigate without going into my head. So...

V: Really, if you're willing to feel what's touched, it all reveals itself. It's only an unwillingness to be with what's being touched that keeps the mind so busy in play, usually trying to escape what the feeling is.

~

S: I used to think that I could just find the silence and that would be enough to begin to wake up, but I feel like it is much more complicated now because that has not really worked for me.

V: Well, I tried every approach known to man because I was interested in the easy way like everyone else is, and there is no easy way. The mind has to be undone and whatever helps or assists with that undoing is worthy. Whatever takes you away from being this way, whatever takes you into dream is not worthy. I kept it very simple. Knowing the ultimate answer was surrender, I had to work out how to surrender, and in working it out, I realised it's not just an understanding of surrender that's required. If you have a whole pile of patterns inside your mind that keep you contracting to life, they're actually hindrances in the way and they need to be undone, and that involves surrendering them, but you can't surrender what you can't see, so you have to examine them to surrender them.

My approach, meditation, allows you detachment from the mind so you can see it. Self- inquiry itself allows you to find Beingness, but finding Beingness in itself isn't going to help that much if you've got a mind that's constantly contracting. In being mindful, we tend to be more present, which allows us also to see more about our own mind. It's in the seeing that we have the invitation to undo it. The seeing is not enough in itself because patterns that have been there for a long time will not just change overnight; they'll continue for a long time unless you intervene. For instance, if you have a belief system that people shouldn't betray you, you're going to have a lot of problems because human beings, by their nature, betray. If every time someone betrays you, you contract and go into resistance, this sort of mind isn't going to be able to support higher consciousness because it's going to go down to lower consciousness every time someone betrays it.

In seeing through that belief and letting it go thoroughly, you no longer get caught on that particular hindrance, but you have to see it and you have to undo it. So yes, it is about finding the silence and stillness – there's no doubt about that, but it doesn't help if you've got a mind that constantly and unconsciously reacts and contracts to things. It has to be undone. A person can sit in satori for years and come out unchanged, and someone betrays them, and they contract again, and they lose satori because they never undid their mind.

S: How did you undo your mind?

V: Meditation gave me the tools to do everything, pretty much. If you meditate, you develop the silent witness that is detached from the mind and you start to see the mechanics of the mind rather than the story of the mind. The story of the mind is about the dramas of life. The mechanics of the mind is why you do what you do: Why do you react? How do you react? And in seeing the how and why, you can start to undo the how and the why and not get caught in contraction. If you can't see the how and the why, you'll never be able to stop it. Seeing through the mind is essential to actually stopping it from contracting.

The other thing I had was really good teachers who kept pointing to what was not working for me and allowing me to have a look at those things and take them apart, and I had teachers from when I was a teenager right through. I spent a lot of time with them and they showed me a great deal about how my mind worked, whether it was good or whether it was bad; whether it was working in favour of freedom or in favour of enslavement. Anything that would contract me, anything that created resistance inside of me became of interest to me. Not the story, but the nuts and bolts of why that was happening; the defence systems that came with the play, the belief systems that supported those defence systems, the expectations that were based on those belief systems. The mechanics of the mind rather than the story of the mind were examined.

One of my teachers talked about the type of enlightenment you can find in a monastery or an ashram compared to the type of enlightenment you find in the marketplace. Someone who wakes up in the monastery where they're totally protected from everything because they don't have to put food on the table or a roof over anyone's head, they're not in relationships so they don't get caught in relationship battles, they may find Beingness through self-inquiry, or through meditation, or through any yogic practice, but can they take what they've found into the marketplace? If they

can't, it's not worth anything. Can you stay in the marketplace and not close while under fire? Because it is a mind that stays open that has equanimity while under fire, that can support enlightenment in the marketplace. When people attack you or have a go at you, it's an opportunity to see: Am I contracting? Am I supporting that contraction? How does that all work? What's going on here? Let's undo this. Not they're right or they're wrong or I'm right or wrong. The nuts and bolts of the contraction, the nuts and bolts of why and how you've lost your equanimity by contracting, until you undo the mind, so it doesn't do that anymore. Then the mind stays open even while being attacked. Does that answer your question?
S: Yes.

~

S: Would you say that an open mind is a silent mind?
V: Pretty much. The more open the mind, the more silent it is.
S: So, how's it possible to respond to others if the mind is so open?
V: Pretty easily. Same as it's easy to ride a push-bike without thinking if you've ridden one before.
S: See, I have this kind of notion. Like for instance, when I talk to you, when you say something to me, it's a bit different from if I was talking to someone in a normal setting.
V: Why?
S: Well in a normal setting, someone says… I think that an intellect comes in or something. There's a reply available, but in a setting like this, the reply isn't necessarily there and could just as easily not be there…
V: Yeah, that's true.
S: So, my point being then, if you have an open mind in an ordinary setting and then you just didn't have that response, then that would mean that you might not know what to say?
V: Yes, possibly, and I'd rather not know than live in my head because in not knowing, just not knowing and being in Beingness, it's so beautiful. Living in the head is not the same, it's not beautiful. It's better to not know, better to live in wonderment, present. Not wonderment as in "la-la land," but wonderment as in being absolutely present without a thought and everything that comes is fresh

because there's no projection. Meditation affords that, so does self-inquiry. You can't think about it, you can't get there through thought or through learning. You can only get there through the practice of abandoning the dream, and the more you practice, the better you get at it, and you lose your acumen, to some degree, in the world because you're not living in your head anymore, but it's a small price to pay for the beauty you find.

S: How did you manage to do your job before you became a teacher?
V: Psychotherapy?
S: The other one.
V: Publishing?
S: No.
V: Naturopathy?
S: Yes, that one. How did you do that without actually thinking it through?
V: Well, I hadn't mastered it at that stage, but you know, I've got books and computers.
S: But you did have to engage your mind?
V: Not a great deal. I was a mechanic as a teenager and could do a job on a car, like change its valves without very much thought at all because it had been done so many times. It's all very repetitive. Mechanics on a car is very similar to being a naturopath because human beings and the treatment of human beings, the diagnosis, is simply mechanics. After a while, you learn the routine and things become automatic rather than a thought process, and so I studied. Studying demanded living in my head to a certain degree because it does, and a lot of study was needed, but I really loved silence and stillness so when I wasn't living in my head because of study, I was actually meditating.

The other side of it is that to diagnose you, I have to listen to you and not while I'm thinking. Silence is needed to listen to you, to feel you, and to get a good diagnosis of what's happening with you. To feel you, I have to be very quiet inside. The job involved being very quiet and very silent to diagnose you because any form of medicine, any form of therapy demands a correct diagnosis. If you don't diagnose correctly, you're off from the beginning. To diagnose you, I have to listen to you, to listen like my life depends on it so I can see where there might be faults, see what is working and what is not working. I practised that form of diagnosis for 10 years, and it was another practice that allowed me to be very silent and very still. That is the right ground for seeing through the mind because you have learned to stop the radio station, learned to quieten it down. You could say that even though it was a job that demanded study, as medicine does, it also demanded silence and stillness for correct diagnosis.

If you'd talked to me long enough back in those days, you wouldn't have to outright tell me what was going on, you'd somehow confess it. The same goes for psychotherapy: if you talk for long enough, you're going to tell me everything needed to work out a diagnosis and then work out a treatment, something that might help. Not a great deal of thought required, just a great deal of listening required. When you listen to another human being, you listen to what they're saying and then you listen to what's under what they're saying and so you get a much better picture, but if your mind is noisy, you only hear what they're saying, you miss what they're saying underneath, you miss what's probably true. It's a bit like hunting in a way. When you hunt, you have to be very quiet. Someone who's diagnosing has to be very quiet because they're hunting the truth about what's going on inside of you, so they'd be very quiet so they can hear. It's pretty hard to deceive someone who's really listening. Another way to enlightenment is to become an ear, just listen, be so quiet, just listen, and then you remove everything that's in the way of listening.

S: With listening, I can see that you'd have to be quite still to listen like that, but then how do you know what to do with what you hear?
V: Well, if you haven't studied, you won't know what you're hearing. It's like you can listen to someone talk in French until the cows come home, but unless you understand French, you won't know what they're saying. You have to learn the language of the body. You have to study the body and its mechanisms; you have to become a mechanic of the body so when you're listening you know what you're hearing. If I put my hand on the motor that's not running

quite right, because of my experience, I could probably tell you what's wrong with that motor. After taking motors apart and putting them back together hundreds of times, the sounds they make are recognised. The same goes with the human body. If you've studied it and you've listened to it, you know what's going on. A doctor can use a stethoscope to listen to your heart and he knows by the sound of your heart what's happening or what's not happening, but if he hasn't studied that, you just hand a stethoscope to someone who's never studied medicine and they listen, they wouldn't know. You have to have some reference points for what you're hearing.

S: If I don't have a teacher or at least a person nearby to act as a clear sounding board, how can I recognise when my mind is moving in a way that is against openness?

V: By observation; you keep observing until it teaches you, if you don't have anyone else to teach you. If something's contracting you, what takes the contraction away? We could look at victim-oriented thinking here. You find that you're contracting and somewhere along the line, you notice that you're blaming – you're in blame mode; you're blaming someone else or you're blaming the situation or you're blaming yourself and you recognise that blaming is why you're contracting. You recognise that being a victim creates contraction in you. Now you have a choice, now you can remove blame, or you can continue to blame. If you're interested in not contracting, you remove blame. Now you've come to that through observing your own mind, you see. If you don't want to contract in life, don't be a victim. It's very simple.

S: You mentioned to keep eyes open when meditating and I noticed that if I was to just sit, close my eyes, or if I'm feeling tired, I go into a dream. So, I understand why the recommendation is there, but why would I go into dream if my eyes are closed? What happens?

V: You're actually not used to not having outside stimulants. You see, if you keep your eyes open, you can stay with something that's real. If you shut them, the chance that you'd be going into dream is quite strong. For people who are beginning as meditators, it's advised that they actually sit with their eyes open at a 45-degree angle downward gaze to help them stay more present to the breath rather than losing it and going into dream somewhere. As a beginner in meditation, and for the first 10 years, I meditated with my eyes open at a 45- degree angle. It was too easy to lose the breath and go into dream when I shut them. Does that make sense? The object of meditation is to be present to what is real; it's not to go to sleep. People look at the Buddhist statues and think it is very spiritual to shut your eyes. Well, if you can shut your eyes and meditate and not go into dream, that's a good way to do it, or you can keep your eyes open or don't bother meditating because it's not working.

S: I'm wondering how can I change my attitude from fitting as much stuff into the day as possible to just being present and meditating, or being peaceful? How do I change my attitude?

V: Okay, so I just didn't give myself a choice.

S: The other day, I had this, there wasn't any thought, but I had this thing occur where I saw we didn't really have thoughts, but instead they are attracted to us. Would you please comment on this?

V: The mind produces thoughts, but if the thoughts aren't entertained, they go away. I don't think they're attracted to us. The mind actually produces them and it has a habit of producing them or a pattern of producing them because they're entertained, and so they just never stop. Meditation, or the abandonment of thoughts, creates a different pattern. The mind stops producing them. The mind's pretty slow though, it takes a while, and it takes a fair bit of practice for that to occur. So, you go back to a stage to where it's similar to being a little child, like a baby, your mind's not producing thoughts any more, but you have an adult mind so you can operate quite smoothly in the world, unlike a baby – it's just patterning. If you have a pattern of entertaining thoughts constantly, well that's what's probably going to happen until you die, unless somehow you start not entertaining thoughts. My interest became silence and stillness, so I wasn't interested in thoughts. I wasn't interested in what I thought. I wasn't interested in my own story. It was just noise. Does that make sense?

As far as the thoughts coming from something attracted to you, I haven't seen that, but you know, I don't know really. Whether they come to you or whether they come from your mind, if you don't entertain them, they go away. The analogy that I used to use

was a pretty good one. If you have a couple of mates drop over at nine o'clock at night and you turn the television on and they like to watch football, so you put the football channel on and you go and get them a pizza and some beers, they're likely to stay. But if you turn the lights out and you don't feed them and you turn the television off, they're likely to go, you know? If you don't entertain the mind, it shuts up after a while, but it does take a while and I'm not going to suggest it's easy. It's not that easy. It just takes a lot of practice. You remember the younger man who was one of my late teachers? He stayed with me in the early 2000s.
S: I never met him.
V: He had this wonderful story. He used to say, "Look, you step in dog shit once, you don't want to ever step in it again." And he said, "You step in the mind once and you see what it's really like, you never want to step in it again." If you truly see what the mind does to you, you don't want to play with it; you just let it go because it's a pain-producing machine. No-mind is so cool.

~

S: You speak about no-mind and also Beingness. What's the difference between them?
V: So, no-mind just simply means that the mind's not talking to itself. No mind. Beingness is what everything appears in. It's the background, pure awareness, and when it becomes aware of itself, that's the satori. If it stays aware of itself, that's enlightenment. The obstacles that seem to be in the way of that are a contracting mind. A mind that is equanimous will support enlightenment. A mind that constantly contracts will not. So, no-mind is best, no-mind means being here without a thought.

~

S: Is no-mind an expansive mind or is it just nothing in it, just clear?
V: So, you get in the car and you turn the radio on and there's noise. You turn the radio off, there's no noise; no-mind, no noise.
S: Is that why there's no preference for pain or pleasure because I think I've heard you say before that there's no preference for either, or not preference, but there's no judgment. Do you not mind if there's pain or pleasure? Why is that?

V: When you start stripping the mind down, you get down to some things that are still hanging around and they're preferences, so you surrender them. It's like anything that's in the way, you throw in the fire, and preferences are in the way, so you throw them on the fire.
S: Is that before enlightenment?
V: It was around about that time. There was a clear sign that preferences were in the way. The best the mind can actually do to support enlightenment is to get out of the way. That's the best it can do.

~

S: When I hear you say, "The best the mind can do is to get out of the way," I recognise that to be a core truth, but something that comes up for me is being grounded and having discipline still activates the mind. Does the mind assist with discipline until I am at that degree where it's a habit that's just so automated that the mind is not needed?
V: Yes.
S: So, the practice of being grounded and having discipline, is that something you cultivated strongly?
V: Yes. When you talk about being grounded, you're talking about being present to something that's real. People who are ungrounded or what we consider ungrounded, are present to their minds and quite often just to their minds. If you're present to the body, you're grounded in the body. If you're present to Beingness, you're grounded in Beingness. If you're present to heart, you're grounded in heart, if you're just present to the mind, you're grounded in the mind and the mind can be swayed all over the place. Where you focus awareness is where you're grounded. Someone who's awake has awareness locked on itself; pure awareness aware of itself.
S: I'm only aware of this present moment, this outward breath now, and yet, my interpretation is that it's my mind. It's my mind using awareness; you're talking about awareness somehow void of mind.
V: Yes, the mind is just a tool you know, that facilitates awareness; being aware of the floor or awareness, being aware of the body or awareness being aware of itself. The mind itself is just a tool, an instrument, and it can be used in a way that supports enlightenment or it can be used in a way that supports dream, depending on what its patterns are.

S: When you talk to me, I get expanded. Is that because your awareness is actually expanded and that is also directed when you speak to me?
V: And that expands your mind.
S: Whereas my practice is still running awareness through the mind because I don't...
V: Your practice is awareness looking outward because awareness looking at the mind is still outward. The sage has awareness looking inward, always.
S: So, unless I develop that inward, inner gaze...
V: Inner gaze, yes. In developing the inner gaze, you become aware of obstacles that stop that inner gaze and this is what I'm talking about tonight – removing the obstacles that stop the inner gaze. The contracting mind stops the inner gaze because it brings awareness back onto itself, strongly. In developing a mind that doesn't contract, it allows awareness to stay on itself. A mind that practises acceptance and surrender becomes equanimous after a while and will support enlightenment.
S: For me to direct that awareness and have an inner gaze, would you recommend being grounded physically?
V: Yes, being grounded in the body is really a healthy thing to do.
S: Is this why some yogis and teachers teach yoga?
V: Yoga grounds you in the body.
S: Part of the path.
V: Yes. When Theravada Buddhists meditate, they walk so they get grounded in their body through walking while watching their breath. There are different ways to be grounded in the body. The body is far more real than the mind; it's not going to disturb you anywhere near as much as the mind.
S: Thank you.

~

S: Are emotions just part of your mind?
V: Sure are.
S: Is there any use in examining them when they arise?
V: Depends on whether they contract you or not. Depends on whether there's resistance or not. If there's no resistance, there's

no problem. It's only when we have resistance in the mind that there's a problem really. Yeah?
S: Is wounding therefore predominantly made up of resistance?
V: It's made up of energy that is held somewhere. It's like a captive, like a prisoner. If there's a willingness to feel it, it can be freed.
S: So, no examination, just feeling?
V: Feeling, yes, the willingness to feel it. We're programmed to avoid pain and to chase pleasure, and so there's this automatic programming that comes into play. For someone to heal their wounds, they have to override that by becoming willing to feel pain or willing to feel discomfort. Surrender, after all, is against the survival mechanism of the body and that's why people don't wake up and stay awake naturally because it's against survival. Someone who has mastered their mind has mastered surrender, which means they have died as an ego, they've gone against the survival mechanism and they've won. They've died. You could say an equanimous mind is a mind that has surrendered.

~

S: Are there times in life where it's necessary to show resistance?
V: Externally yes, but internally no. Like, for instance, say when raising children, you have to put firm boundaries in place from time to time, but can you do that from a place of openness internally rather than a place of resistance? Sometimes you have to read the riot act to people who might be stepping over the line. Can you do that from a place of openness or are you going to contract and go to resistance inside? In the beginning, when you learn to be open internally, it is hard to put up boundaries. It takes practice because we are accustomed to putting up a boundary and going into a defensive mode internally by contracting. To learn to stay open while putting up firm boundaries outside takes a fair bit of practice over quite a period of time.

~

S: If I go to put out a boundary, I find I can't get…
V: Your mind's gone? Okay. Whatever we practise, we get good at. If you practise openness, you will become good at it. If all you do is practise resistance to life, that's all you'll ever be good at. It's very simple. The practice of openness is actually against survival, that's why it's

so difficult. It is in our best interest for survival to practise closing, but if we're interested in higher consciousness, it is the practice of openness that takes us to the sky, not the practice of resistance.

S: Are you saying that being fearful is resistance?

V: Indeed, it is, and when fear arises, we can support that fear, or not support it. There's a choice there. After all, fear is not real. There's nothing real about fear. It's a mind trick.

S: So, fear is created?

V: It is indeed. It's a projection. It's not real. It might seem real, but it is not.

S: So, there's no reality to fear. Is it worth examining?

V: Fear is a survival mechanism. As a matter of fact, fear is your main survival mechanism. Without fear, you'd probably be dead, but as an adult, we can learn to live in the world without fear by just remembering to be careful. You don't get on the bike and do 200km an hour. You don't need fear to remind you, you know you're going to get yourself killed if you do.

S: So when fear arises, you focus on something else?

V: You just don't support it. As you become more conscious, you see it arising and you see the opportunity not to support it, or you can support it, but I don't think there's an advantage in supporting fear. It ruins your life; it stops you from playing.

S: What do you mean by "it's a projection"?

V: Well, there's nothing real about it, it's a projection to the future. We're not frightened of the past, we're frightened of what's going to happen in the future. It's nothing to do with now; it's to do with a future projection. It's living in the future, which is not living in the now; it's living in the dream of the future and an unpleasant dream. Fear is not a pleasant phenomenon.

S: What would cause you to have more fear one day than another?

V: That's a great question. Where do you find the answer? If you could let me know, that'd be awesome. Investigate yourself and see why. Why is it so? Lift the rocks and have a look underneath, become an explorer of your own mind, make it an inward adventure.

Well, I think that's it. Thank you for Satsang. Good to see you brave hearts here tonight.

What Happens in Enlightenment?

V: What are the things that humans don't seem to get, even though the evidence is already there? Everything that you have got is going to be taken off you. People have this dream that somehow it isn't going to happen to them, or it is going to happen later. Everything you have got is going to be taken off you and for as long as you resist, you suffer. The main cause of suffering is attachment, the unwillingness to let go, and as long as we are unwilling to let go, we stay in kind of a dream, a projection of a before and a later. We don't stay in reality – it keeps us in a dream.

After teaching acceptance for about 25 years now, there haven't been many people yet who have heard or understood because their acceptance is an intellectual understanding and when it's actually put to the test, it's usually conditional. They will accept "If…." True acceptance is not conditional, it's like surrender. True surrender is not conditional, so people continue to resist life instead of accepting it and continue to suffer when what they're attached to gets threatened or taken away. Even though you think you're hearing me right now, I doubt there is anyone in this room who can hear me right now.

You see, if you understand, truly understand the Four Noble Truths; first that life is dissatisfying, second that dissatisfaction is caused by desire and attachment, third that there can be an end to this, and fourth, that there is a pathway out, an Eightfold Path – if you understand it, you're not going to stay asleep anymore. You'll do everything within your power to get free. You'll do everything like a man would do who is underwater, starving for air, to get to the surface to get air. You are dreaming, and you think that somehow you have a later. It is a dream. There is no later, there is now. The sage lives in the moment. Ego- based people very rarely own the moment – they live in a dream, which they think is real. It's made up of projections and memories. There is absolutely nothing real about it. You're living in an illusion created by your own minds.

I have you do martial arts sometimes because when you have a sword in your hand and you're being faced by an opponent and you're in the thick of battle, you come into the moment temporarily. The sage is in that moment every moment, day or night. The sage isn't in dream because the sage is awake.

If you're thinking about what's being said, you're dreaming. It can penetrate without thinking. Meditation and mindfulness and the practice of openness can bring you to reality, nothing else. You can't think your way into reality. As long as you resist what is, you will suffer, and your resistance to what is will not change anything. Whatever happens, happens. Your suffering will make no difference whatsoever. When you start living in the moment and you're interested in truth, what you truly are becomes self-evident, but your dream has to drop.

Unconditional surrender is the dropping of the dream.

~

S: Why can't I truly hear you?
V: You're asleep. You're lost in dream. You project onto me that you think you know who I am to start with, and you don't have a clue who I am. What's looking at you is the universe without a mask. The human brain can barely comprehend what it is; the brain is much too limited.

~

S: You said that we couldn't hear you and I felt like I could hear what you're saying, but there's like a veneer or a layer of something stopping me.
V: Yes, it's a defence system; it's what Lao Tzu referred to as impenetrable ignorance.
S: So even in wanting to hear what you're saying, it's not enough?
V: No, you're not willing to pay the price to get out of the dream. Who you think you are dies, no later, no before, no future, no past, no identity; gone.
S: You've done some work with me recently on getting rid of my identity, but I feel like I just find a new one, or I find a new way of feeling okay.
V: That's because you never practise surrendering, you practise coping mechanisms.

S: So, I think I'm practising…
V: That's a thought, it's not a truth. With true surrender, there is no continuation – it's a full stop. In the dream, there's always a continuation, there's always a later in a dream, not in reality. All these teachers who are telling people how easy it is, telling people that they're almost awake, this is a lie. You have to die as an "I". That's the deal, and then who you really are becomes self-evident. You're attached to your life, you're attached to your future, you're probably attached to your partner, you're probably attached to your money, you're probably attached to your property, you're probably attached to a dozen things that you won't let go of, and when those things are threatened or when those things are taken away from you, you're probably going to suffer.
S: When you talk about dying, I notice that I do have attachment to all the things you are saying, and it feels like…
V: You're not listening to me; nothing I've said has landed in you yet. See, when something lands in a person, I feel it go in, it devastates them. Nothing has touched you because nothing has landed, all I keep hitting is a wall of impenetrable ignorance and I know it.
~
S: When you started the discourse talking about attachment…
V: Attachment causes suffering, with desires. You look at what a desire is, desiring something to be different than how it is and then you attach to that, it's the attachment to that, not necessarily the desire, the attachment to the result. Someone who is awake can desire something, but there's no attachment to it, so there's no suffering in it. People get attached to wanting to be heard and suffer when they're not. They get attached to wanting not to be betrayed; they suffer when they're betrayed because they have an attachment to a result. It's all about attachment, the suffering.
S2: So how did you dismantle the pattern?
V: I died. I was willing to. I was willing to give my life for truth, which meant I wasn't going to make it, I was going to die, and I knew that.
S2: Is the death of the "I" a slow process?
V: No, it's pretty sudden. It happened as a result of satoris, as a result of a willingness to stop, a willingness to be annihilated, a

willingness to be in pain forever, a willingness not to be in control anymore. The ego, which is not who you are, is simply a survival mechanism that insists on controlling so it won't die, that's all it is, it's not you. It has nothing to do with you actually, you're already there. It's superimposed on top of you and it thinks it is you, but it's not, it belongs to the animal. You're not the animal either.

S3: You just said you're not the animal?

V: No.

S3: My identification, my experience of recognising the traumatic experiences is the animal.

V: That's right, it's the animal.

S3: It just dropped on me that I identify with the animal.

V: Yes, you do, and you're not the animal, you never have been. What you are can't be born, and it can't die.

~

S: I've heard you talk about not being attached to your kids or your wife. How did that happen, was it just detachment?

V: No, it was a death. My wife noticed after about a week that she had lost her husband. Vishrant had gone.

S: Is it a yes to letting go?

V: It's a yes to death. It's a yes to death. Death is the letting go of control completely. Thy will be done, not my will. I seem like you, but you live as a contraction and I live as expansion. Contraction is ego-based reality, expansion is being-based reality, and they are nothing alike. I can't even really say expansion, there's just nothing here; vast nothingness.

You see, if you understood the Four Noble Truths, why would you suffer? It's like the person in an insane asylum banging their head against the wall. If they knew they were hurting themselves they would stop, but they don't. They don't know because they're deluded into thinking something else is happening.

There is no future, and there is no past, there is only now. Yet you drag your past with you constantly and you project it and parts of it into the future, thinking that in the future it's going to be the same, which is also delusional because it's not true, there's nothing true about it. You can't base a future on past events and past projections because everything is changing constantly. All you can say is it's your best guess if you're honest, but it's not real in any way, shape or form. Without any projections, without any memories, who are you? What are you? This is just a meat suit, it's not who I am, it's not who you are. What's in the suit, what's really in the suit? Beyond psychology, that's what Mystery School is about: beyond the mind, beyond this meat suit, beyond. Gate, gate, para gate; gone, gone, gone beyond.

~

S: When you spoke to me earlier, you put your hand on my back and said "die" and it hit me what's required; that let go of control. I hold onto control so tightly and it's like I let go, but I don't really let go because I hold onto it at the same time.
V: That's right, because you don't want to let go. I wanted to let go.
S: Is it because I don't recognise the suffering...
V: You just don't want to let go. It's how it is.
S: What makes someone want to let go?
V: Consciousness. How conscious are you? I was conscious enough to see it's the only way out.
S2: I've heard you say you knew the deal was death.
V: Yes.

~

S: It feels like a very deadly discourse tonight.
V: Deadly discourse. I'm here as a lighthouse, right? To wake the sleepyheads up, but you keep putting bloody blindfolds on. You pull the wool over your own eyes. You think the story is real. Every time you go into your story, you're pulling the wool over your own eyes, and you're blinding yourself to reality, every time. There's nothing happening.

~

S: Yes, I am seeing where I hold on so much around money. If I feel like I'm going backwards financially I do not want to go there, there's this holding, this not wanting to let go. I can feel this grasp around survival.
V: You can let go and still move forward financially. You don't have to hold on, you know?

S: How do you actually let go of that demand and just be free of that grasp?
V: Have you got a $100 dollar note on you? Has anyone got a match? [LAUGHTER]
S: How do you just let go of it without having to burn money? What can I do?
V: If you're holding onto barbed wire and it was being dragged between your hands, would you hold onto it?
S: No.
V: Why?
S: Because it's painful.
V: And you can see that's what's happening, right?
S: Yes.
V: You can't see what you're doing. You're too unconscious to see that you're holding on is like holding onto barbed wire that's being drawn through your hands. You're too unconscious to see what's happening. Any form of attachment is going to hurt you and anything you're attached to is, sooner or later, going to get threatened or taken off you, sooner or later. That's how it is, that's what this plane is like for every human being.

~

S: Your discourse felt very powerful tonight and this thing about attachment being the cause of all suffering, I like it in those terms because it seems so simple and obvious.
V: You'll forget.
S: Yes, I do.
V: People do, they forget.
S: Yes, I've heard it before in this way, you've given discourses about attachment and I'm like "Yeah, of course." I liked when you said you can have a desire, but it's the attachment to the outcome that causes the suffering.
V: Yes.
S: How can I better hear you?
V: Listen like your life depends on it, because it actually does.

~

S: How do I see more deeply the Four Noble Truths?

V: If you understand the Four Noble Truths and you're still resisting life, then you do not understand the Four Noble Truths. Because if you knew that suffering is caused by attachment and you continued to get attached and resist when an attachment is threatened, then you haven't understood the Four Noble Truths, because if you really understood them, then you wouldn't resist.
S: So, how do I understand them?
V: You would need to contemplate them much more deeply than you have, and it might dawn on you that this life is suffering and there is only one way out. The thing that suffers has to die and the thing that suffers is the one that wants to resist.

~

S: How do you wholeheartedly engage in life and be detached at the same time?
V: How does an actor play a convincing part knowing full well it has nothing to do with him or her?
S: To me, there is some level of identification almost to do it that well.
V: Everything that's happening here right now is an act. Everyone here is acting, everyone is pretending to be a student, and I'm pretending to be a guru. It's a big pretence. It's just that I know it is a pretence and you don't because you think it's real, you think you are the student.

~

S: I feel disillusioned with myself, like I put on this kind of act, this jovial act I use as a defence, and it seems very unconscious. If I go into a social scenario, I'll be like "I'm not going to use spiky humour, I'll just be genuine," but 10 minutes in and I'm straight back into it and underneath it is a heap of low self-worth and it feels like there is no point to life.
V: Wow, that's true. So, if there's no point to life and you're still here, what are you going to do?
S: My thing has always been, in my head, I'll give my life to truth. It's always been my thing, but it's like, I'll wake up every day and I'll give my life to work or whatever else. It's hitting me how unconscious I am.

V: So, giving yourself to truth is pretty difficult unless you're nearly awake, right? I didn't give myself to truth until I was nearly awake. What I did, 11 years before is, I gave my life to heart, which is pretty easy to do because you just work out what heart would do and then you do that. It's pretty simple. Heart would have you being in service to the planet, to humans, to animals, to everything. That's the way of the heart. That will annihilate you as an "I" and prepare you for truth. I serve heart, and I serve truth, and if you're helping me, you're helping serve heart and truth. So, I helped my teachers whenever possible because that was helping serve heart and truth. Someone who is awake is a lighthouse for others. They sacrifice their lives to be awake. Otherwise, they wouldn't be awake. As a result, they can be a lighthouse to others, they're in service.

~

S: You said to me the other day that I was quite wounded.
V: Really? That must have shocked you! [LAUGHTER]
S: It didn't really shock me, but where would you say my wounding lies the most... where am I most unwilling to go?
V: That's really not for me to just tell you that, it's your job to find that out. You're a man, you're not a child, you have to investigate for yourself – only children get spoon-fed. You have to discover for yourself through your own endeavours, through your own efforts, like a man.

~

S: With not wanting to let go of the past or the future, I feel like I need to hold onto that to be effective.
V: Well, you hang onto it, that's best. I'm here for people who want to be free, not for people who want to hang on.
S: I'm always thinking there is a tomorrow or later.
V: Yes, in many religions that are generally about enlightenment, one of the reasons people don't wake up is because they're putting it off until later, always later, postponement, postponement, next life, you know? As long as you have that attitude, you won't wake up. It has to be now.
S: It's been my experience that the willingness only comes when you start to get out of the way, like I don't see that the "I" becomes willing.

V: Yes, it does. You just haven't seen it, so you don't think it exists.

~

S: I feel very expansive.

V: That's nice. Your path is a devotional path; you shouldn't stop your devotion. It's what's going to open you up and set you free. A lot of Westerners can't be devotional because it's too embarrassing for them, but you followed a devotional path because you come from a country where the people are devotional. Don't give it up because it's your path to freedom. I was devotional like you were, and I'm a Westerner.

S: I get attached to my kids.

V: Yes, they are very hard to let go of. The hardest thing for me to let go of was actually my children, but I knew the deal: internally you can't hold onto anything. You care for and love them, but you need to be able to let go.

S: When I hear you tonight, it reminds me of putting truth first.

V: Once again, I don't think you should do that. I think you should put heart first. I don't think you're close enough to put truth first. People who are close to truth are finding themselves in Beingness all the time; they are flipping in and out of satori all the time. Then you put truth first because it's really obvious to you, it's not a concept. If it's a concept you can't put it first, it has to be the real deal. So, you serve heart first, and in heart, you'll become less than. As you become less than, you'll find yourself more as truth.

~

S: During your discourse talking about attachment, it struck me a bit deeper when you said everything you have, you'll lose, and just in that second when you said it, I saw this huge construction of dream I have around the future of everything, even possessions, inanimate objects.

V: Yes, you and every other human on this planet, but you see it.

S: Yes, just that second of "Wow, my life is like a raft."

V: A raft of dream, which keeps you away from reality.

S: Yes, and then soon after that was a pang of fear, when I realised I will lose everything. So, I can see that the raft keeps me away from…

V: It keeps you away from the fear of annihilation.

S: It feels so immense; how much I'm attached to that I could lose. I could only handle a small knock of loss and then I can rebound off that by focusing on everything else.
V: Yeah, how about losing everything?
S: Yes, so how do you lose everything and make everything okay?
V: Give yourself no choice. A disciplined mind gives itself no choice.
S: You mentioned you will lose everything and there will be no choice.
V: You're going to anyway and you're going to lose it sooner than you think.
S: But is it at that point whether you can struggle or…
V: There's a possibility at that stage; if you're with someone who's awake, there's a possibility that you may wake up. When you see that you're losing it all, there's a possibility.
S: How much of a possibility?
V: If you're with someone who's awake, there is. Someone who is awake can take you in that surrendered moment, into Beingness.
S: Just before death, really?
V: Just before death, yes.
S: I had a counselling session on Saturday and I'm still going through some stuff. We went through some things and I noticed a deep feeling of not being acceptable to others.
V: And is that okay?
S: I'm trying to make it okay.
V: Well, that's your job, that's right. Make it okay to be unacceptable, that's your job and where you're caught and why you can't make it okay is because you're not willing to wear the consequences of being unacceptable – which means abandonment and rejection. Make abandonment and rejection okay, and you'll be able to be okay with not being acceptable, okay?
S: Thank you Vish.

~

S: Today I went back to the house where I had been living before I moved up here. I had underestimated all the stuff I left behind. A lot of it was boxes of photographs and things from my wedding and things that mum owns, and things that were all associated with memories that were quite sad, and loss…

V: Yes.
S: And just understanding how much I suppressed my past.
V: Suppressed it or left it behind?
S: I tried to push it away.
V: Suppressed it or left it behind though? You see, we don't need to carry the past with us.
S: I think I told myself that I had left it behind, but I had actually hidden it in boxes and put it in places where I couldn't see it.
V: You know, in 1987, I burnt everything; tapes, clothes, photographs, everything.
S: I threw away all my old wedding photos today and things where I'm just holding onto the past.
V: Yeah.
S: I also had a counselling session yesterday and did some work around parts.
V: Parts?
S: Parts, just identifying a part of myself.
V: Oh yeah.
S: When I was throwing things out today there was the part that was aware that I didn't need to hold onto those things, but there was a harshness to throwing these things out.
V: Yeah, I discovered I didn't actually have to burn anything, all I had to do was let it go. [LAUGHTER] Anything else?
S: No, thank you. [LAUGHTER]

~

S: Whenever I speak to people about Buddhism, one of the most misunderstood statements is that desire and attachment is the cause of suffering.
V: Yes.
S: You were talking about attachment earlier, and with attachment, so many people seem to interpret it as, "Don't ever allow yourself to feel close to something because then it will hurt if it gets threatened," hence attachment causes suffering.
V: Well, what about owning things? Don't ever get attached to them because they're going to get taken away from you. What is it like? It's like if you touch the iron when it's on, it's going to burn you, and somehow people don't get that.

S: So, how does that look?

V: From where I am, insanity because people keep touching the iron!

S: But how would someone just not have attachments.

V: The "I" has to die.

S: So, is it not possible to practise?

V: It is possible, but as long as the "I" is there, it will be running true to its nature. The "I" is programmed for survival; attachment is a part of survival.

S: Does it leave you dispassionate?

V: Can do, can do.

S: How can you tell the difference between actually letting go and closing down so you don't feel anything around people close to you?

V: I don't understand the question.

S: Would someone who closes down very easily assume that they are not being attached to things?

V: Well, they are closed down, aren't they? See there's the difference, closure.

S: That's one of the criticisms I've heard about Buddhism, it's like, "Oh no, don't ever desire anything; don't get close to people, that's attachment." Sort of equating it to closure.

V: Yeah, well that's not true, that's just a misunderstanding. Get rid of the "I".

We are One

V: You've just sung a song and some of the words are "We are one," and for a lot of people that's a concept, just a mental understanding. For those who have found themselves as truth, it is actually how they live. In Beingness, there is no sense of any separation. For those who are awake this is true because it's not a mental concept, it is known in the moment, it is happening right now.

There is only one, there is no two. There is no such thing as duality. That is just a mind trip. What we are, our true nature, is not separate, it is one; coming from one, through a body and a mind to talk to you. I talk to you as though I am separate because I use English to speak to you and English is a language designed for the ego. It is a language that actually creates separation, but you would not be able to understand me if I were to talk to you from my true nature, because a lot of you actually don't have ears to hear yet. My true nature is silent, and it is still, and this is the case for you too, but you haven't recognised or realised this. Even if you've had satoris and you hold it in memory, it is nothing like being aware of it in this moment.

Enlightenment is knowing yourself as truth, which is one. No separation, no two, one. So, when awareness goes very far back, very deep into Beingness, there is only one. I can come out here and meet you in this dream world, but it is a dream world that you believe to be real. You take away your projections and your memory and then you may be able to get in touch with your true nature, which is not dream. The past is just a memory that is not real. The future is a projection which is not real. Your analysing is not real. What is real is Beingness. Everything appears in it and is part of it and everything disappears in it. We are one.

The invitation is to tune in to what's here and find your own true nature. The invitation is to join me instead of me having to constantly join you in the dream world. In reality, there is actually nothing happening. There is just vast nothingness or everything-ness. Whichever way you want to put it, you're pretending to be a somebody because you believe you are, but without your imagination, who are you? What are you? Without your imagined past and your projected future, without your analysing, your dreaming, what are you? Who are you? Because you're not that, I'm not really trying to help you find peace, you already are that. If anything, I'm trying to break down what is not real so you can discover what is real. You resist this.

Many times in 21 years of teaching, people have asked me to tell them what I can see. 99.9999 per cent of the time I will not do that because the person who has asked is not ready to see. Sometimes, I've actually made the mistake of telling the person what I could see, and they have run away because they weren't ready to hear. Their ego didn't have enough strength in it to handle the truth. This game is a game of destruction; destruction of that which is false to leave what is real. Everything you think is false; everything you think you are is also false. Make no mistake. Unconditional surrender is the annihilation of who you think you are.

Any questions, any statements, any challenges to this teaching this evening?

~

S: You just said that you don't tell people what you can see because their ego doesn't have enough strength in it. Are you talking about the character to be open towards what is being shown?
V: I show people what they are ready to see. People deserve the truth, but if they're not ready to see, then there's no point in showing it. It takes a willingness to be annihilated. When the Buddha sat under the Bodhi tree and surrendered unconditionally, he was annihilated as an "I", that's why awakening occurred. You can't learn your way to enlightenment. That's not possible because it's not the mind that becomes enlightened. The mind facilitates it, but it does not become enlightened.
S: You were speaking about the statement that we are one. Prior to enlightenment, did you have a concept of that?
V: I knew it to be the truth because it had been experienced in satori 11 years before, but it was only held in memory.
S: Things like that or karma, past lives and so on, is there much value in trying to understand them?

V: Take away the dream and you are free. You see, most humans think they are the body, which is a spacesuit that has an onboard computer for the spacesuit, but it is not who we are. Most people think they're that because they're ignorant of their true nature. Enlightenment in Buddhist terms is the end of ignorance.

S: How is it even possible if there are flip-floppers or people who have had satoris in this life... how does the ego get deluded again even after seeing that it is not the identified mind?

V: The ego doesn't actually want to die, so it uses its experience of Beingness to survive by pretending to be awake.

~

S: Sometimes, I feel the inability to wake up because I compare myself to you. I feel like you are very effective in the material world and I am not very good so acceptance seems harder. Regardless of how effective I am in the material world, if I completely accept how I am, as ineffective as I might be, can awakening still occur?

V: Awakening occurs because of unconditional surrender, not acceptance.

S: How is acceptance different from unconditional surrender?

V: Acceptance is milder; unconditional surrender is death. In acceptance, the ego can survive; in unconditional surrender, the ego dies.

S: Acceptance is a stepping stone?

V: It's a stepping stone.

S: Is surrender a conscious choice in the moment or is it an automatic thing if you know how to do it?

V: It's not really a choice, it's a non-doing, it's an end. It's a ceasing of all activity, it is a full stop, it is a non-doing. My mind is not moving, it's dead still, it's not doing. You could say that the mind is surrendered.

~

S: The other day, my mind was empty, but then different thoughts would arise, so I practised trying to let them go. Is that the best that the mind could do – just try to let go of the thoughts?

V: Yes, that's the best it could do. It can practise letting go of the dream for something that is real and that is mindfulness and meditation.

S: I did a Nadabrahma meditation tonight and now I feel high as a kite, really spacious. I equate this to when I've done an extended period of some sort of spiritual practice. If I haven't, then I don't feel like this. You don't do anything, so I find it invaluable how you stay in some form of higher clarity.

V: I'm awake, that's all. My mind doesn't have an interest in itself; therefore I'm present to reality every moment.

S: So, it's because I think that it doesn't stay like this for me?

V: Well awareness goes back to the thoughts, goes back particularly to the contractions. If somebody needs to practise, then they're not awake; they are still ego-based.

S2: I also did a Nadabrahma meditation tonight, and I felt great. Then it got lost when I realised that I was going to be late to come here because I contracted. Then something realised what was happening, so I let go and came back to the moment, but it kept coming up. So, how do I stop that contraction before it even happens?

V: You'll have to be more conscious than you currently are.

S2: Is that just through the practice of meditation?

V: If you become interested in the mechanics of the mind rather than the story of the mind, you can become more conscious of the mind's activity. As long as you remain interested in the story, you are lost in lower consciousness.

S2: So, is that why I'm contracting?

V: I don't know why you're contracting. You're the one who needs to know that.

S2: Yes.

~

S: You mentioned the other day that the house has to be empty as an analogy.

V: Yes.

S: Is it also that the emptier we are, the more density, with regards to energy, is flowing in?

V: That's a possibility, yes.

S: So, to keep the house empty, or to keep empty, is it just not having any belief systems and the clearing happens by itself or do we need a practice of clearing?

V: The story of you keeps the house full. There's an interesting story about a seeker who climbs a mountain to see a sage. It's a very arduous task. It takes all day to climb the mountain and when he gets there, he sits in front of the sage and starts asking him questions and starts telling the sage what he's seen and what his life's been like and what wonderful insights he's had. The sage starts pouring him a cup of tea and the seeker keeps talking, the sage keeps pouring. After a while, the cup fills and starts to overrun into the saucer and the seeker says, "Stop, you're overfilling my teacup!" and the sage says, "Yes. This teacup is so much like you. You are too full for me to pour any more into. You are too full for me to pour anything into you. To show you anything, you need to empty first." When Osho told this story, he said also, not only do you need to empty the cup, you need to break it, and I agree. That way, nothing can ever get caught in you again; there's no place. Then the world can pass through you. Satsang is a process of destruction. People who come here to collect more knowledge for their ego are missing the point of being here. Anything else?
S: No. Thank you.

~

S: When you speak about unconditional surrender, was it the same as you used to practise when you were younger and you were a fighter?
V: Yes, similar.
S: So, what was your practice?
V: I always went into a fight, into combat, to win, but also prepared to die. I wasn't going to save myself at the cost of losing; if you want to win, you've got to be prepared to die. If you try to protect yourself too much, if you're too fearful of death, you can't play. The fear itself will haze you, it will slow you down, and it will defeat you. It is said that there's nothing to fear, but fear itself. It's true and there's nothing real about fear, it's just a projection, but people believe the projection to be real, so they get caught in it.
S: When you say, "There's nothing to fear, but fear itself," to have that understanding, do you need to have no preferences?
V: How do you hunt an animal?

S: Quietly?

V: Yes, but you watch it. You watch its mannerisms, its habits. If you want to understand fear you hunt it, you watch it, you watch its mannerisms; you learn all you can about it and you'll discover in that learning that fear is not real, that it is simply a projection. There's nothing at all real about fear.

S: But if there's a fear there, do you just have to be okay with the worst outcome?

V: If you want to be. I just never considered it; I just refused to serve fear. I refused to serve something that wasn't real.

~

V: I'm playing with the energy in the room. If you're sensitive enough, you can feel it pulling you into silence. When people move and create an energy, it disturbs what's happening here. Just because I'm looking at this and looking at that doesn't mean I'm not playing with the energy here; it's happening. Anyone who's sensitive enough can feel it. Satsang has begun, as a matter of fact, any time you come anywhere near me, you'll feel it because inside of me is awareness on awareness. That creates a silent screen, and if you are energy sensitive enough, it can wipe your mind, it can take you into Beingness, and it can enlighten you. In Pune days, if you moved around disturbingly you would have been banned for a week. Papaji used to sometimes come into Satsang, pick up a newspaper and read or watch the cricket for hours because he was trying to get rid of the people who thought Satsang is about words.

It's not about words, it's about silence and stillness, and Beingness emanates it. Tune in and you'll find it here, day and night. That is what it's like inside of me all the time and that is your goal; to be like that also.

~

V: In the business of higher consciousness, most teachers are snake-oil salesmen: they're not actually telling the truth, or they are telling borrowed truths that they don't fully understand. If you tune in here, you'll start to find the stillness and the silence; you will start to find your own true nature. It has nothing to do with ideologies or beliefs. It has nothing to do with understanding. It has nothing to do with your mind because you are not your mind, before your mind is pure awareness. You are that, you have always been that, you cannot be other than that. The belief that you are a somebody is a misunderstanding. It is not correct. Take away your imagination and that understanding of who you think you are cannot exist, it can only exist in your imagination. Yet, you can be aware of your true nature every moment; Beingness, I am, without the "I". This is the goal of Buddhism, this is the goal of Hinduism, this is the goal of Sufism and Taoism; to know yourself as Beingness, to know yourself as truth.

S: You say that "Tender okay-ness with everything that arises" is a complete teaching.

V: Yes, that's done from the mind; it's the ego that supplies the tenderness.

S: So, how is that different from that space then?

V: Consciousness is not the ego. Ego is actually unconsciousness, it's a dream. There's nothing conscious about the ego. The difference is between reality and non-reality. Beingness is real, ego is not. It can't be, it's a dream. Take away your imagination and it doesn't exist. If you think you know better than your teacher, and you do, it's time to find another teacher. If you actually practise what is taught here, you will wake up. The teachings of Vishrant are the teachings of the masters from the last 2500 years in Buddhism. None of the teachings that are taught here are mine – that's not a possibility. They are all 2500 to 5000 years old and they are the same teachings that have awoken most of the people who have woken up.

Of course, if you don't practise the teachings, you won't wake up. If you don't practise being present, you won't be present. If you practise thinking about it, you'll be practised at dreaming. That doesn't raise your consciousness levels one bit. Reality doesn't have any give in it. It is either real or not real. There are no shades, there is no fluffiness to it, it's straight; it's either true or it's not true.

S: So what's higher consciousness?

V: Well, that's what the consciousness of Beingness really is. True higher consciousness is knowing yourself as truth. Sometimes it's called super consciousness, but true higher consciousness is knowing yourself as Beingness and then you have the lower consciousness basically under that. Anything that involves dreaming is lower consciousness. In the New Age religion, they think higher consciousness is dreaming, but it's not; true higher consciousness is knowing yourself as truth. Anything that involves dream, any form of dream whatsoever, is lower consciousness. Of course, there are different degrees of lower consciousness. So, someone who is having a mild dream is in a relatively higher point of lower consciousness. Someone who is angry is lost in lower consciousness, absolutely lost in lower consciousness. It's one of the reasons you should never support anger.

~

S: With consciousness higher or lower, you said you can raise your consciousness levels from lower consciousness to higher consciousness?

V: You can only raise your consciousness levels by getting out of your head. Meditation, mindfulness, and self-enquiry are the practices that will raise your consciousness levels. Learning about the scriptures, learning about Buddhism, learning about Hinduism, learning about Sufism or Taoism doesn't take you to enlightenment. It is only practice that takes us to higher consciousness, nothing else. If you're living in your head, if you're a head dweller, you're living in lower consciousness. No matter what you think, you are living in lower consciousness. From lower consciousness, you can be very quick, you can be very clear sometimes, but you are no match for someone living in higher consciousness, you're no match at all. Dream doesn't have a chance against reality.

S2: Is it the same in the upper levels of martial arts?

V: At the top levels of martial arts, if you're thinking, you've already lost.

~

S: This "two teachers" thing has been a real trip for people over the years.

V: It has been.

S: Because of language use and methodology clash.

V: Well, people are looking for an easy way. They are trying to learn their way to higher consciousness by listening to YouTube videos and reading books. No YouTube video will lift your consciousness level, not really. Educating yourself doesn't work. There's only one thing a person needs to know: surrender, unconditional surrender. If you know that, you've learnt everything you've ever needed to learn.

~

S: I like how you always address everything and don't leave any stones unturned and I like the way you set people up for truth and talk about truth and how you challenge people on Facebook; if you don't agree with something, you will tell them.

V: They don't like that, quite often they unfriend me. [LAUGHTER] The world doesn't like the truth much, I assure you. They like their cosy little warm lies.

S: It really highlights to me that you will talk the truth, no matter what.

V: Yeah, there was some enlightened organization claiming that Sat-Chit-Ananda means meditation. It doesn't mean meditation, it's a description of an enlightened person, it's a description of Beingness, and I pointed that out to them.

S: So, the problems with listening to other teachers and having other teachers, mostly seems that when there are clashes in the teachings, the ego looks for a way out, ways to make you wrong.

V: There were teachers when I first started teaching telling people that they were awake when they weren't. Some of the waves of neo-Advaita Vedanta teachers of the last few decades were telling people they didn't need to meditate!

S: Yeah, there are so many little clashes that the ego latches onto. I've seen so many people bring in other teachers' teachings that they would use against you. So, how would you deal with that?

V: Of course, challenges are welcome, but ultimately, if you're with a teacher and you're a student, you come as a student, not a know-it-all, otherwise, you need to go.

~
S: I feel like I protect the fear of insanity with arrogance because if I'm wrong, then I can't trust my own mind.
V: Well, you can't trust your own mind. Who programmed you?
S: Not me.
V: That's right. So, who programmed you?
S: My parents and society.
V: And how balanced are they?
S: Not very.
V: Right [LAUGHTER] My own mind has been referred to affectionately as the "bullshitter" for 21 years now. It's not believed at all, because of who programmed it.
S: You asked someone earlier, "How can students handle situations well if they don't fully understand what is going on?" And your answer was to ask questions.
V: Well, that's what a student does. A student asks questions because you have to assume that the teacher knows more than you, you have to. If you can't assume that, you need to find another teacher. If the teacher knows more than you, then you ask questions until you can find out what they know. That's the correct way to proceed.
~
S: I liked your Satsang last night on satori, and coming in and sitting with you this morning, it's just instantly silence and there is such beauty. Last night, you said to me to just meditate. Is that the only way for a student to find that sort of space with a teacher?
V: Pretty much. I used to find that space in meditation every time because I used to meditate for long periods. I found that space of no-mind, that space of detachment. I had absolutely no interest in what my mind wanted to talk about, no interest. I was in love with the silence and stillness.
S: I remember once you said that you thought that you needed to sit in that long enough and then it would...
V: ... it would take in Beingness, not in no-mind, in Beingness, it's just not true. The reason people stay awake? I don't think anyone knows the answer to that question. Every teacher I've ever heard talk about it, talks about grace, and to me, when a teacher talks

about grace they're talking about "they don't know". [LAUGHTER] They sound so spiritual and holy when they say it though.
S: You said your mind is programmed by parents and society.
V: Well, my mind was programmed to be a war machine; programmed to be a winner at all costs, nasty, not very good for the heart. I was sent to the top schools in Western Australia to learn how to win at the cost of everyone else.
S: So, my question is, you have re-programmed yourself a lot...
V: ...de-programmed, not re-programmed.
S: ...yes de-programmed yourself a lot. So, does that make your mind any more trustworthy than it was before?
V: Silence and stillness is trusted. The inner knowing is also trusted, but that's not the mind, it's something else beyond the mind, I don't know what that is. The analytical mind is not trusted.
S: So, even with good programming it's still dishonest?
V: Tends to be because a part of its ability to survive is the ability to deceive. Unfortunately, it deceives itself. A lot of people think things about themselves that just aren't true, like some people think they are actually good friends to other people when the truth is, they are actually bad friends because they won't tell other people the truth.

~

S: Is inner knowing an impulse or is it just somewhere you find yourself when you realise that inner knowing has taken you there?
V: Inner knowing is the weirdest thing in the world because you can't work it out actually. Sitting Bull, a leader of the North American Indians, outran the cavalry for many years with his tribe. He could feel them, he knew they were coming. That's inner knowing. He knew where they were going to attack, without information, without intelligence, he knew. That's inner knowing. He was a shaman and a chief; he lived in the energy world. You can't comprehend it. It's not analytical.
S: I like it when you say, "trust your inner knowing".
V: It's hard to get in touch with the inner knowing. Most people listen to their ego and sometimes, if they understand what inner knowing is, the ego pretends to be inner knowing. The thing about inner knowing is it just knows, it doesn't in any way try to convince you,

it doesn't repeat itself, and it is always really, really, really quiet; it just knows, whilst the ego has a different way of presenting itself.
S: How can you tell the difference between what is the ego and what is inner knowing?
V: You have to become quiet, you have to become quiet. You have to quiet the noisy mind.

~

S: I feel a lot of low self-worth being touched, but it's not so much that I feel low self-worth, but things are just touching me and there is a sense of me being a failure.
V: Then you should try harder at being a nice person.
S: Yeah…
V: No, no, yes. You see, you should try more at being a nice person, and what it will do is eliminate your ego. Different people do different things. Openness will eliminate your ego, but for you, being a nice person will eliminate you as an I.
S: I do try to be nice.
V: Yeah, but not to your husband.
S: Yeah, I do try as well.
V: Yes, there is a difference between trying and doing. "Don't try, do" – Yoda.

~

S: Regarding the two teachers thing: I have been studying and reading up on Buddhism for four or five years and I have never been with a teacher; you are the first teacher I have sat with.
V: Well, there aren't many teachers, not really. Not in Western Australia.
S: Well, I was over east, but even then….
V: Not even over there, because it is an eastern religion and the Ajahns in the monasteries keep most of their teachings for the monks. They don't really do a great deal of teaching to the general public, and if they do, it is watered down. It's watered down a lot.
S: I still like to read teachings from some Buddhist Ajahns.
V: Sure, you'll find the teachings are very similar.
S: Yeah, I've read this book of reflections quite a few times, and after sitting with you, I've been reading it again and I identify with a lot of similarities.

V: About 25 years ago, I went to Murdoch University – I think I have told you. I studied there for six months, reading all the old teachers; they all say the same thing, it's always the same thing. It always boils down to surrender.
S: I kind of see the Buddha as my teacher, but he died a long time ago.
V: So long ago.
S: I don't know if that's helpful.
V: His teachings were good, but he was a man of his time and some of his teachings aren't as appropriate anymore because times are different. That's why I have given away the strictness around celibacy, I don't think it appropriate. In Australia, it can be difficult if monks aren't allowed to handle money because you can be arrested for vagrancy. Also, needing to beg for a living doesn't work in the same way here as it is illegal to beg across much of Australia. The rules around these things and how to do them were sensible rules in their day, but it's not relevant anymore.
S: Yes, I find it inspiring to read about other people's experiences, and I usually do it before I sit down and meditate. It sort of gets me ready for my work day and it's inspiring. So, even though they're not my experiences, knowing that they are possible, gives me some sense of joy.
V: You want some joy, a spoonful or just a little bit? [LAUGHTER]
S: Is it a helpful way of using books?
V: If you study Buddhist teachers, you'll find that most of the teachings are the same as here anyway. It's when you start looking at teachers from neo-Advaita Vedanta, which you're not into, and you find there are a lot of clashes in the teachings. So a while back, I started stopping people from really getting too involved with these other teachers because it was just headaches. This teacher says that, that teacher says this, is this right? Is that right? It makes it difficult. With Buddhist teachers, they all say the same thing. They all say meditate, and be mindful, which is okay, you know. There's not much of a clash in Buddhism, it's when we step outside Buddhism that the clashes begin.
S: You chose Buddhism to practise or to teach?

V: Yes, but ultimately I am not a Buddhist.

S: Because you're a nothing.

V: Yes, a nothing, that's right, Nirvana. As a nothing, there's no identity. There's no clash with any of the Buddhist teachers in Australia because, apart from celibacy, they pretty much teach the same thing. If on the other hand, you were to start studying neo-Advaita Vedanta, you would have problems. I think most of these neo-Advaita Vedanta teachers are just super salesmen who have found temporary Beingness through self-enquiry and who are making money out of people's ignorance.

S: One other question that I have, you talk about three types of energy?

V: Yes, in Hinduism there are three gunas. Three types of energy; tamasic, which is the sleepy, lethargic, lazy, unconscious type of energy; rajasic, which is change, action, movement, and can be irritable, angry and restless. Then there is sattvic, which is pristine, clear, silent, still, bright. The aim is to go to sattvic. So in Hinduism, even the food, the clothing, the music they listen to, it is all categorised by these three gunas, depending on what it brings you to. In Ayurvedic medicine, the three gunas are involved, the three different styles, and it's a whole methodology towards enlightenment, but it has seeped into Buddhism to some degree, pure mind; sattvic. You want to have cloudiness, you get the tamasic and a little bit of rajasic together and you have a lot of cloudiness and it's not so cool. So, the idea is to lift yourself above tamasic and you do that through rajas.

Rajas is watching the breath, that's action. You see, watching the breath is action, it lifts you out of tamas, it lifts you out of the dream, and then from rajas, you can sit silently, but that's a much later stage. The first stage is to lift yourself out of tamas, out of the dream, and you do that through rajas, through watching the breath. Once that is achieved, once that is a default as a meditator, you can go beyond that and you just sit silently with no watcher, nothing. Just here in no-mind, in nothingness, there are different stages.

It is quite hard for people to actually learn to meditate because they are so used to having a noisy mind; so untamed, so out of control.

S: Yes, that is my direct experience.
V: Yes, but if you keep playing, if you keep playing the game, you start enjoying no-mind, you start enjoying the silence and stillness. You'll start finding it; you'll start looking for it. It's just that probably your whole life you have enjoyed the noise; you've enjoyed analysing, looking at things and thinking. That's okay, it's just a habit now, and it's in the way. So now you start to develop a new habit of enjoying the openness, and the spaciousness, and the silence, and the stillness and the reality of the world rather than what you think about the world. What is that? This is Buddhism [LAUGHTER] Basically, Basic Buddhism.

I don't teach "ritualised" Buddhist religion. What we are teaching here is fundamental, real Buddhism. This is a way of life, not a set of belief systems, superstitions or rituals. This is what actually works. I sometimes challenge people's understandings, beliefs and superstitions around Buddhism, and if they look and question themselves, it can be quite good.

~

S: I have a question about arrogance.
V: Would you like some? [LAUGHTER]
S: So, if I have arrogance in me, but maybe it's not showing itself...
V: Passive arrogance; well, that would be typical because you are a passive-aggressive person, so your arrogance would be passive as well, wouldn't it? "I know better than you, but I'm not going to tell you because you might hurt me." I'm sure that's not how you think... "I'm not going to tell you because I'm superior to you." That's more like it, yeah? [LAUGHTER]
S: So how do I get rid of that?
V: Keep bringing it up with me and I'll make as much fun of you as I can. [LAUGHTER] You're here to have your eyes open, and that's actually what's happening, and when you get absolutely thoroughly sick of yourself, you might move to change.

~

S: In the past, other people, I can't remember who, have used other teachers' teachings to either discredit you or make themselves right.

V: Yeah, they have tried. They haven't done very well.
S: Is that just human nature?
V: The problem is people aren't real students. You see, a real student comes to find out the truth and they are willing to be a student. Someone who comes with their own ideas and thinks they already have knowledge is actually not a student, they're something else, but they're not a student. So you get people who come along to prove themselves because they have a spiritual ego as a seeker, and so they are looking to prove themselves with me, but they can't because I'm not here to support the spiritual ego. As a matter of fact, I am here to destroy it so they can be free, so they fight for their imprisonment – they fight for their spiritual ego.

~

S: You said you are pointing things out to people to make them sick of themselves?
V: Sometimes, it depends if that's what they need or not.
S: Some things have been pointed out to me for years, but I still haven't really looked at it too much.
V: Well, it won't change then, if it's a hindrance or an obstacle then it's going to stay there isn't it?
S: Yes. Just thinking, "I can go on just how I am."
V: Really? Bill Murray huh? (Reference to the movie Groundhog Day)
S: [LAUGHTER] And then things will change by themselves.
V: They won't. You know what's going to change the most, don't you? You're going to get old.

~

S: Communication has been the thing I have been getting feedback on, from everyone, and now with employees, it's…
V: …imperative.
S: So looking at communicating as clearly as possible, but I noticed this new employee we have got, has a habit to smile every time and say "Yes, yes, yes, yes," but you can see that he still hasn't got it, but you're being as clear as you can.
V: Uh-huh. No, what you do is ask them to repeat it back to you and see if they understand.

S: Every time?

V: Yes, and ask them to repeat it back to you and see if you think they have understood what you're talking about. Otherwise, you're going to have mistakes. Every time I ring up the local Thai restaurant for Thai food, I ask them to repeat back the order, because sometimes they say "yes" when they don't understand, you know? So, I get them to repeat it back and that's the best way. That way, we don't get the wrong food, or less of the right food or more. If you're dealing with people who don't comprehend, then you have to make sure they comprehend, otherwise, it will cost you money.

S: And you have to do it every time?

V: Well, until you actually work out how to read the guy properly. You know? It's a learning curve on your part to learn how to deal with him, and what he can and can't understand, what his comprehension levels are, and that takes time. In the meantime, you need to get it right every time, so you need to check. Isn't that so?

S: That's right. At the moment, you turn your back and then when you go back, he has done it the wrong way.

V: Is he competent?

S: He is really nice and is really competent, once he has got it, and then he is really good.

V: Okay. Well, you just need to load up the machine properly.
[LAUGHTER]

~

S: You spoke about having two teachers. The only other teacher I have ever looked at was Eckhart Tolle in the early days, not so much these days, but he did speak about the problem with having more than one teacher.

V: He did, yeah. Robert Adams spoke about it quite strongly, dealing with two teachers is just difficult, people get different ideas.

~

S: I remember getting agitated when we listened to different psychological videos and at the end, you would criticize them and then I would be like, "Oh, come on!" I don't know, I think it touched something in me. Then I would spend the next hour defending that person [LAUGHTER] So, that's like a characteristic

I see in you, it's like, you look at something and quite quickly you will...umm...

V: ...Challenge it? This gives you the impetus to have a look rather than just accepting everything. I challenge you to look, I challenge you to have a look to see what's going on rather than just accepting everything. I challenge you to look, I challenge you to find, to see what's going on rather than just being a drone and going along with everything anyone says.

S: That's sort of, I don't know if opinionated is the right word... **V:** Yes, but if you're trying to prove me wrong, you'll be looking, will you not?

S: Trying to prove you wrong...?

V: Yes, if I'm criticizing someone and you think I may be wrong, then you'll start looking, won't you? You'll start examining it. **S:** Yes.

V: Then I've got you doing what I want you to do, having a look.

[LAUGHTER]

~

S: What I see with the guy I work with is that he has got ideas of what it means to be a man; he has got all these things about being free, as kind of an ego, like he doesn't accept people telling him what to do.

V: A true man is someone who is in service to everyone because he is a caretaker. A true mature man is in service. This idea of freedom you're mentioning? Free from what? Free from responsibility from taking care of everyone?

~

> *"Take away your ears and hear me.*
> *Take away your eyes and see me.*
> *Take away your mind and be me, I am you."*
>
> VISHRANT

About Vishrant

Vishrant is a contemporary mystic who offers a pragmatic path to higher consciousness. He made a fortune in publishing as a young man, retiring at the age of 28, and as a world traveller and student of personal development later met controversial Indian guru and spiritual teacher Bhagwan "Osho" Shree Rajneesh who initiated him into the world of higher consciousness and enlightenment.

That encounter led to Vishrant tasting unconditional love during a terrifying shipwreck off the Western Australian coast and then glimpsing his own true nature. After these revelations, he shocked everyone by giving his multi-million dollar company to the staff who had served him so diligently for a decade, before then setting off around Australia barefoot for the next four years while searching for how to open his Heart once and forever.

After Osho's death in 1990, Vishrant committed himself to the Way of the Heart while working as a naturopath and psychotherapist, running men's encounter groups and later serving a crop of Advaita Vedanta teachers who started visiting Western Australia at the end of the 1990s. Vishrant woke up in 1999 in the presence of one of those teachers.

Since then, Vishrant has held satsang and retreats, and runs a Mystery School in the Perth hills which is also available online for those seeking to find their true nature.

Vishrant's teachings are pragmatic and free of belief systems and religious ideologies. He sees himself as a reality teacher rather than a spiritual teacher and says spirituality has become an overused word. His invitation is for people to investigate the Truth through their own direct experience.

To get involved, visit vishrant.org.

www.ingramcontent.com/pod-product-compliance
Lightning Source LLC
Chambersburg PA
CBHW030551080526
44585CB00012B/342